Gallery Books
Editor Peter Fallon
CHOSEN LIGHTS

CHOSEN LIGHTS

*Poets on poems
by John Montague*

Edited by Peter Fallon

Gallery Books

Chosen Lights
was first published
in a clothbound edition
on the occasion of
John Montague's 80th birthday,
28 February 2009.
Revised edition 2013.

The Gallery Press
Loughcrew
Oldcastle
County Meath
Ireland

www.gallerypress.com

ISBN 978 1 85235 563 0

A CIP catalogue record for this book
is available from the British Library.

The Gallery Press acknowledges the assistance
of The Ireland Funds in the reissue of this book.

Contents

Poems by John Montague
     Essays by various authors

Preface

'The poet who survives is the one to celebrate, the human being who confronts darkness and defeats it is the one to admire.' By Donald Hall's yardstick John Montague, on the occasion of his 80th birthday (28 February 2009), more than half a century after the publication of *Forms of Exile*, has earned a right to our applause.

We at The Gallery Press have been publishing John's poetry since 1988, following his long alliance with Liam Miller and Dolmen Press. *Collected Poems* (1995) was the first apogee of our association. I wrote then of it, his life's work to that point: 'part self-portrait, it is even more a "landscape with figures" — and it has the look of a masterpiece'. Since then we have published two new collections and we discuss others, including a round-up of his French translations.

Frequently Festschrifts remain tied to their occasion so, to mark the milestone of John's birthday, we decided to invite an assembly of poets who have published books with The Gallery Press to select one of his poems and to outline a claim for its worth in their estimation and affection. There was an immediate and enthusiastic welcome for the idea. To discover, in particular, young poets' first encounters with poems and/or collections was both enlightening and corroborative. (We regret that a number of John's peers, despite their best wishes, felt unable to participate.)

I wondered if certain phases of the work — early? middle? recent? — or, indeed, if the 'greatest hits' would attract or inhibit responses. Our book offers evidence that John Montague has admirers of all ages for all stages and registers of his work. It is a remarkable testimony that the essays respond to poems from each of his published collections.

Individual choices seem both uncanny and natural — Michael Longley's of 'Windharp', with its 'heatherbells and ferns', a poem I imagine he'd be proud to have written himself; Eavan Boland's of 'A Lost Tradition'; Ciaran Carson's of 'The Country Fiddler'; or Michael Coady's (with *his* passion for music) of 'O Riada's Farewell'. Derek Mahon gravitated towards one of John's 'eco-poems', Frank McGuinness to one that embraces a theme of Ibsen's, while the most recent conscript to Gallery's list, Ciaran Berry who now lives in New York, attends to 'A Graveyard in Queens'.

Chosen Lights could be called a democratically determined *Selected Poems*. It is a book which provides insight into a plethora of poets' methods and interests and a storehouse of critical insight and personal remembrance. Above all, we hope it serves to honour an artist of uncommon dedication and ambition, a maker of enduring poems. It's long since some of his lines and phrases entered the consciousness of Ireland. We salute a poet who is, as Eamon Grennan concludes, 'a marvellous, marvel-making force that for all these years has won the admiration, affection and gratitude of so many of us'.

Peter Fallon

CHOSEN LIGHTS

The Water Carrier

Twice daily I carried water from the spring,
Morning before leaving for school, and evening;
Balanced as a fulcrum between two buckets.

A bramble-rough path ran to the river
Where you stepped carefully across slime-topped stones,
With corners abraded as bleakly white as bones.

At the widening pool (for washing and cattle)
Minute fish flickered as you dipped,
Circling to fill, with rust-tinged water.

The second or enamel bucket was for spring water
Which, after racing through a rushy meadow,
Came bubbling in a broken drain-pipe,

Corroded wafer thin with rust.
It ran so pure and cold, it fell
Like manacles of ice on the wrists.

You stood until the bucket brimmed
Inhaling the musty smell of unpicked berries,
That heavy greenness fostered by water.

Recovering the scene, I had hoped to stylize it,
Like the portrait of an Egyptian water carrier:
But pause, entranced by slight but memoried life.

I sometimes come to take the water there,
Not as return or refuge, but some pure thing,
Some living source, half-imagined and half-real,

Pulses in the fictive water that I feel.

Poisoned Lands (1961)

Justin Quinn *The Water Carrier*

Yves Bonnefoy's sequence 'La maison natale' begins with the statement: 'Je m'éveillai, c'était la maison natale', and in the following sections he repeats this moment of waking in the house where he was born. We keep returning to childhood for our various reasons — psychoanalysis, art, public justification, nostalgia. It is both a source and resource. It is protean in that it changes its demeanour, shading and outlines each time we go back to it. We make it say what we want it to say, not what it would tell us, on each occasion. As a subject for poetry it is particularly treacherous, because when we return to it we are more likely to encounter Wordsworth than our younger selves, a stylized view of early events, rather than the events themselves. Poetic structures can sometimes seem too willingly to hand, the epiphanies prefabricated and suspect.

John Montague's 'The Water Carrier' is a report from the poet's rural childhood, from pre-industrial Ireland, a country without running water, television and electricity, a country which imposed daily rhythms and natural encounters that are rare today. It would seem to guarantee some kind of authenticity (that is, if one finds the present somehow inauthentic). What is engaging about the poem is that it refuses hackneyed consolations; that it insists that the water, and indeed the whole experience, is 'fictive', and, with the final image of water running through the child's hands, that it is also ungraspable, unusable. Granted, the 'halfs' of the penultimate line are straight out of Wordsworth, and some of the other diction suggests authenticity, but phrases like 'pure thing' and 'living source' are curiously vacant of meaning, and all we are left with at the poem's end is the poet uncertain as to how such experience might be slotted into larger structures (perhaps structures of autobiography and the nation, as evidenced in Montague's other work). The speaker might indeed physically 'feel' the water at the end, but he also tells us that this immediate sense experience is not true: it is invented, created, fabricated, 'fictive'. As that last word sends beautiful suggestions rippling outwards through the stylized scene (for he *has* stylized the scene, despite his asser-tion to the contrary), we can observe other freedoms as they offer themselves to the poet. It is an exhilarating moment.

Like Dolmens round my Childhood, the Old People

Like dolmens round my childhood, the old people.

Jamie MacCrystal sang to himself,
A broken song without tune, without words;
He tipped me a penny every pension day,
Fed kindly crusts to winter birds.
When he died, his cottage was robbed,
Mattress and money-box torn and searched.
Only the corpse they didn't disturb.

Maggie Owens was surrounded by animals,
A mongrel bitch and shivering pups,
Even in her bedroom a she-goat cried.
She was a well of gossip defile,
Fanged chronicler of a whole countryside;
Reputed a witch, all I could find
Was her lonely need to deride.

The Nialls lived along a mountain lane
Where heather bells bloomed, clumps of foxglove.
All were blind, with Blind Pension and Wireless.
Dead eyes serpent-flickered as one entered
To shelter from a downpour of mountain rain.
Crickets chirped under the rocking hearthstone
Until the muddy sun shone out again.

Mary Moore lived in a crumbling gatehouse,
Famous as Pisa for its leaning gable.
Bag-apron and boots, she tramped the fields
Driving lean cattle from a miry stable.
A by-word for fierceness, she fell asleep
Over love stories, *Red Star* and *Red Circle*
Dreamed of gypsy love-rites, by firelight sealed.

Wild Billy Eagleson married a Catholic servant girl
When all his Loyal family passed on:
We danced round him shouting 'To hell with King Billy',
And dodged from the arc of his flailing blackthorn.
Forsaken by both creeds, he showed little concern
Until the Orange drums banged past in the summer
And bowler and sash aggressively shone.

Curate and doctor trudged to attend them,
Through knee-deep snow, through summer heat,
From main road to lane to broken path,
Gulping the mountain air with painful breath.
Sometimes they were found by neighbours,
Silent keepers of a smokeless hearth,
Suddenly cast in the mould of death.

Ancient Ireland, indeed! I was reared by her bedside,
The rune and the chant, evil eye and averted head,
Fomorian fierceness of family and local feud.
Gaunt figures of fear and of friendliness,
For years they trespassed on my dreams,
Until once, in a standing circle of stones,
I felt their shadows pass

Into that dark permanence of ancient forms.

Poisoned Lands (1961)
and *The Rough Field (1972)*

Alan Gillis *Like Dolmens round my Childhood, the Old People*

First and foremost, the poem strikes the reader with its vivid picture-painting and story telling. There's a dead-on precision and shrewd economy at work, but also a steady, lilting measure. The writing's flow is naturalistic, yet the stanza's structure is totemic. Montague's first five stanzas each give us a character, a sense of milieu, and repeated flashes of such bewildered insight as we get from Maggie Owens' 'lonely need to deride', mingled with the feral otherness of her fangs. When we're told 'Jamie MacCrystal sang to himself, / A broken song without tune', and that he 'Fed kindly crusts to winter birds', the speed and neutrality with which we're then informed 'When he died, his cottage was robbed, / Mattress and money-box torn and searched', leaves an indelible impression. In this way, Montague creates an iconic verisimilitude. Each textured and dynamic portrait irrepressibly pulls the reader in. The poem's seven stanzas, each seven lines long, create a hefty sense of solidity, while they teem with potency and action.

The independent opening line and closing lines, which sit apart as preface and conclusion, are key to Montague's poem. Their apartness creates the effect of the poem's unforgettable ending:

> *Gaunt figures of fear and of friendliness,*
> *For years they trespassed on my dreams,*
> *Until once, in a standing circle of stones,*
> *I felt their shadows pass*
>
> *Into that dark permanence of ancient forms.*

But these opening and closing lines also form a binding ring around the poem's seven solid stanzas. At the end, as the shadows of the gaunt figures pass into 'that dark permanence of ancient forms', we are led straight back to the beginning, where the old people are 'like dolmens' — permanent and ancient forms. It's as if the intervening stanzas are being gathered into a circle.

Given that the seven stanzas depict a rather bustling and antagonistic sense of these characters and their milieu, it might seem as if, at the poem's end, they are passing into some form of relief and redemption: transfigured into unfallen symbols, monumentalized in a mythological present. Yet what happens is more fully compelling. There is no hygienic simplification of the scene. Rather, it is the stanzas in their fullness — the entire complex and paradoxical, harsh but vivacious reality — which pass into 'that dark permanence'. Because of the poem's in-built loop, its circular structure, its stanzas are already exemplars of the 'dark permanence of ancient forms'. Therefore, these ancient forms, this dark permanence, is not static or purified, but is instead the very stuff of contradiction. While the living become megalithic, this is no petrifaction. The dolmens are not at peace; the poem's stanzas are its dolmens, and they writhe and burst with violent life.

The final turn of the screw comes from that great gap between 'I felt their shadows pass', and the final line. Through what do the shadows pass? What is the nature of this gap? In one sense, the past, the shadows, have passed through you, the reader. A communal but vanishing history — with all the gradients of gentleness and viciousness contained in the poem — has passed through you into that 'dark permanence' which exists, unsettled, somewhere both within and beyond you.

Soon enough, this monumental poem will be fifty years old. It has surely been one of the most influential Irish poems of its time. Few readers who enter its circle, now and in the future, will escape its elemental imprint on the imagination. It passes into the spirit. It grows each year.

A Welcoming Party

Wie war das möglich?

That final newsreel of the war:
A welcoming party of almost shades
Met us at the cinema door
Clicking what remained of their heels.

From nests of bodies like hatching eggs
Flickered insectlike hands and legs
And rose an ululation, terrible, shy;
Children conjugating the verb 'to die'.

One clamoured mutely of love
From a mouth like a burnt glove;
Others upheld hands bleak as begging bowls
Claiming the small change of our souls.

Some smiled at us as protectors.
Can those bones live?
Our parochial brand of innocence
Was all we had to give.

To be always at the periphery of incident
Gave my childhood its Irish dimension; drama of unevent:
Yet doves of mercy, as doves of air,
Can falter here as anywhere.

That long dead Sunday in Armagh
I learnt one meaning of total war
And went home to my Christian school
To belt a football through the air.

Poisoned Lands (1961)
and *Time in Armagh (1993)*

Gerald Dawe *A Welcoming Party*

How was that possible?

I first heard about it from my mother who had watched the same newsreel in the Capitol cinema on the Antrim Road in north Belfast. People thought at first, she said, it was some kind of a B-list horror movie, 'made-up', and then as reality dawned, others got sick, screamed, left the cinema in a state of shock and revulsion.

When she told me about it I must have been about the age she was (or a little younger) when she saw that newsreel, and it stuck with me — her impressionable youth, in the house of dreams, where she and her girl friends went twice weekly, before and during the war, when Belfast had a palace of dreams on every main road, where that Pathé film made the impact it did, caught between horror and disbelief. In 'Autobiographies' Derek Mahon imagines a similar time:

> *Gracie Fields on the radio!*
> *Americans in the art-deco*
> *Milk bars! The released Jews*
> *Blinking in shocked sunlight . . .*

John Montague likewise records in his sequence of poems, *Time in Armagh*, heavily influenced by World War 2, the older poet's view of his growing up 'at the periphery of incident'. The sequence is scored with war — 'A bomber's moon' that brings destruction to Belfast (the Blitz of 1941) or, in 'Waiting', 'the camp where German / Prisoners were kept', 'the guard towers rising, aloof / As goalposts', leads, 'years later' to 'another camp — / Rudshofen, in the fragrant Vosges —'

> *The stockade where they knelt the difficult,*
> *The laboratory for minor experiments,*
> *The crematorium for Jews and gypsies*
> *Under four elegant pine towers, like minarets.*

In his recollection 'The smell of woodshavings' . . . from the German prisoners of his childhood 'plugs / My nostrils' with the adult experience of 'a carrion stench'.

Elsewhere in *Time in Armagh* history stalks the corridors of memory only to emerge in 'A Welcoming Party' with the starkest of images of human degradation and the pitiless vision of 'That final newsreel of the war':

> *From nests of bodies like hatching eggs*
> *Flickered insectlike hands and legs*
> *And rose an ululation, terrible, shy;*
> *Children conjugating the verb, 'to die'.*

The contradictory beat of Montague's poem captures the dual life of that time — as war comes to an end, the civilian victims of the Holocaust are released but life cannot return to normal:

> *That long dead Sunday in Armagh*
> *I learnt one meaning of total war*
> *And went home to my Christian school*
> *To belt a football through the air.*

'A Welcoming Party' is a powerful, humbling poem in its truthfulness, depicting the meaning of 'our parochial brand of innocence' as 'all we had to give'.

In Dedication

My love, while we talked
They removed the roof. Then
They started on the walls,
Panes of glass uprooting
From timber, like teeth.
But you spoke calmly on,
Your example of courtesy
Compelling me to reply.
When we reached the last
Syllable, nearly accepting
Our positions, I saw that
The floorboards were gone:
It was clay we stood upon.

A Chosen Light (1967)

Dermot Healy *In Dedication*

In the *Collected Poems* of John Montague this poem appears under the title 'In Dedication' at the beginning of 'All Legendary Obstacles' in the collection *A Chosen Light*. On the internet I found it under the title 'Uprooting' and since the act of leaving home, and up and going, is at the root of some of John's poems I chose this short verse because it seamlessly strips bare, not only language, but love and identity, and the sense of place.

He is tilling sorrow, as the Afghan quotation states at the beginning of *The Rough Field*, with great simplicity and truth. And the body, which carries on with life, is itself heading back, despite all its knowledge and awareness, via the ruin of a house, to its skeletal origins, as is echoed in the second verse of 'Cassandra's Answer', a later poem, published in *Mount Eagle* where one of the themes of 'uprooting' is returned to:

> *To step inside a childhood home,*
> *tattered rafters that the dawn*
> *leaks through, brings awareness*
>
> *Bleaker than any you have known.*
> *Whole albums of Births, Marriages,*
> *roomfuls of tears and loving confidences*
>
> *Gone as if the air has swallowed them;*
> *stairs which climb towards nothing,*
> *walls hosed down to flaking stone:*
>
> *you were born inside a skeleton.*

The sense of a ruin that housed a family is beautifully caught in the above verse, and this same fever of loss permeates 'In Dedication', but here it is also a loving personal relationship that is going, down through the floors, to the last *s* on the tongue, and yet the lady's sense of bravery and courtesy means the poet is obliged to carry on till acceptance arrives for them both, as they approach silence.

First the roof goes, lastly the floor beneath the feet, and in between the walls and the glass are all filched. The descent starts as they converse in the everyday. 'My love', the poet begins his dedication. The address is quiet. Intimacy laces the opening, as slowly we step into the lift to travel to the bottom floor. We are going down. The attempt is to soldier on as the portents grow more ominous. The conversation bravely continues and then the sounds begin to die out. As you descend what you pass disappears. And, at the last stop, as we step out, Montague has allowed us a beautiful rhyme:

> The floorboards were gone:
> It was clay we stood upon.

This is an earth rich with loneliness and acceptance. Over our heads are the exposed rafters. The decorations are in shards. The time together near over. The walls weigh heavy. The lad who was searching for a home finds the man in him leaving a ruin behind, that once housed the familiar and the loving.

Everything has been uprooted.

Who they are that removed the roof are never named. They, again nameless, in time will start on the walls. They could be the spirits of fate, but despite the dismantling, behind the scenes Montague, through his sense of loss, is taking on the obstacles and rebuilding the ruins, from the first foundation stones, to the stairs going from floor to floor, up to final ceiling. Loss is at work with great intensity and simplicity. Then the journey ends. We are faced into emptiness, but the ground is at our feet.

The poet touches the core when he speaks of reaching 'the last syllable'.

The silence is all pervading.

The Trout

for Barrie Cooke

Flat on the bank I parted
Rushes to ease my hands
In the water without a ripple
And tilt them slowly downstream
To where he lay, tendril-light,
In his fluid sensual dream.

Bodiless lord of creation,
I hung briefly above him
Savouring my own absence,
Senses expanding in the slow
Motion, the photographic calm
That grows before action.

As the curve of my hands
Swung under his body
He surged, with visible pleasure.
I was so preternaturally close
I could count every stipple
But still cast no shadow, until

The two palms crossed in a cage
Under the lightly pulsing gills.
Then (entering my own enlarged
Shape, which rode on the water)
I gripped. To this day I can
Taste his terror on my hands.

A Chosen Light (1967)

Paul Muldoon *The Trout*

Not only did I read 'The Trout' while a student at Saint Patrick's College, Armagh, which was the same school John Montague had himself attended, but I read it under the spell of Jerry Hicks, one of the same teachers who had taught Montague to read poetry only twenty years earlier.

I recognized, even then, something of the long tradition of Irish nature poetry to which 'The Trout' belonged and in which Hicks was so immersed. Indeed, a trout appears in Irish literature as early as a seventh-century poem, surfacing there as *iasc brecc*, the speckled or spotted fish. The term *breac-Ghaeltacht* would have been one with which Hicks was all too familiar since it refers to the speckled or spotted geographical areas in which Gaelic- and English-speakers were interspersed. One such 'brackish' area where the saltwater had almost been displaced by the fresh was in County Tyrone, not far from where Montague had lived as a child, and where Hicks had collected songs from some of the last native Gaelic speakers in Northern Ireland. Montague refers to this phenomenon in 'A Lost Tradition':

> *The last Gaelic speaker in the parish*
> *When I stammered my school Irish*
> *One Sunday after mass, crinkled*
> *A rusty litany of praise:*
> Tá an Ghaeilge againn arís.

In this same poem, Montague refers to having gone to primary 'school / In the Glen of the Hazels', a reference to the Tyrone place name Glencull, or *Gleann Chuill*. Another 'hazel wood' in the vicinity of Coole, County Galway, comes to mind, complete with the stream in which Aengus 'caught a little silver trout' that would shortly become 'a glimmering girl':

> *I will find out where she has gone,*
> *And kiss her lips and take her hands;*
> *And walk among long dappled grass.*

The 'hand' of 'The Song of Wandering Aengus' reaches for the 'hands' of 'The Trout', while 'dappled' is picked up in 'stipple'. Other than the perfect rhyme on 'hands' itself, there's only one full rhyme in 'The Trout'. The far-flung, perhaps unconscious, rhyme on 'stipple' and 'ripple' brings to mind 'nipple', a word one might associate with the erotic 'glimmering girl' in Yeats.

Another Yeatsian echo is 'bodiless'. It's a term Yeats uses in 'The Symbolic System', an essay on Blake in which he describes how a poem begins with a '*bodiless* mood' which then becomes a 'surging thought' before emerging as a 'thing'. I think Montague is alluding directly to Yeats when he describes how the trout '*surged* with visible pleasure', while the thingness of 'The Trout' also puts Montague directly in touch with his other early example, William Carlos Williams, and his mantra of 'no ideas but in things'. Though I used the word 'erotic' earlier, I should modify that to 'autoerotic', since what enters the speaker's 'own *enlarged* / Shape, which *rode* on the water' turns out to be his own 'thing', the word having been used by everyone from Chaucer through Shakespeare to the autoerotically-gifted boys in the class in Saint Patrick's College, to refer to the 'penis'. The underlying sexuality of the poem probably deserves an essay in itself, particularly since the lines 'the two palms crossed in a cage / Under the lightly pulsing gills' summons not only a literary father (the bard of Lough *Gill*) but Montague's actual father, who just happens to be the subject of a poem entitled 'The *Cage*', in which the son describes his subway-worker father 'released from his grille / in the Clark Street I.R.T.' and connects the 'pulse' of 'The Trout' with 'the mark of an old car / accident *beating* on his / ghostly forehead'.

All Legendary Obstacles

All legendary obstacles lay between
Us, the long imaginary plain,
The monstrous ruck of mountains
And, swinging across the night,
Flooding the Sacramento, San Joaquin,
The hissing drift of winter rain.

All day I waited, shifting
Nervously from station to bar
As I saw another train sail
By, the San Francisco Chief or
Golden Gate, water dripping
From great flanged wheels.

At midnight you came, pale
Above the negro porter's lamp.
I was too blind with rain
And doubt to speak, but
Reached from the platform
Until our chilled hands met.

You had been travelling for days
With an old lady, who marked
A neat circle on the glass
With her glove, to watch us
Move into the wet darkness
Kissing, still unable to speak.

A Chosen Light (1967)

Gerard Smyth *All Legendary Obstacles*

John Montague's 1989 collection *New Selected Poems* is notable for its abundant grouping of so many of John's perfectly formed shorter poems, each of which has the poet keeping faith with what he himself once termed the 'fierce lyric truth'.

It is a book replete with some of the finest examples of the supple music John achieves — as well as his rigorous and exact clarity — when dealing with his major themes and preoccupations: love, ancestral landscape, remembrance of the past, family history and his consistent interrogation of Ireland's troubled and troublesome wider national history.

All of these familiar themes are rendered with that combination of exquisitely crafted imagery and meditative attention to the inner voice that sets his work apart. To pluck any single poem from this over-arching, richly representative selection is therefore difficult. But it is in the love poems — always closely focused — and in the love poet's acute sensibility, that I sense his 'fiercest' adherence to that lyric truth. The much-admired, frequently-anthologized 'All Legendary Obstacles', in its four tightly controlled stanzas, is a compound of all the fundamentals of the archetypal, and exemplary, Montague lyric: the spare architecture, the sensuous cadence, and on occasion, the wistful melancholy. From image to image, the mood — tender, expectant — is sustained by Montague's powerfully imaginative transformation of an ordinary event: the reuniting of the two lovers.

'All Legendary Obstacles' is another of those Montague poems that demonstrates the candour the poet has always been capable of. Yet it also epitomizes his knack of allowing candour and restraint to work hand-in-hand. There is an almost cinematic quality to the sequence of images in their unfaltering progression towards the final and private moment when lover and beloved keep their rendezvous and

> *Move into the wet darkness*
> *Kissing, still unable to speak.*

The moment is preserved with strikingly effective simplicity. That vividly atmospheric 'wet darkness' is a perfect conclusion to a poem in which 'the hissing drift of winter rain' has already been set down as a central motif. The sensory effect of 'flanged' is wonderful in '. . . water dripping / From great flanged wheels', while the description in stanza two of the poet 'shifting / Nervously from station to bar' signals the palpable anticipation at the heart of the poem.

Here again, as in so many of his Irish poems, John recognizes the power of place names, introducing Sacramento and San Joaquin with their evocative local resonances. The legendary obstacles themselves — 'the long imaginary plain' and 'monstrous ruck of mountains' — create a dramatic sense of the expansive American landscape and the distance of separation that has necessitated the beloved 'travelling for days'.

'All Legendary Obstacles' stands among John's most memorable poems because in the making of it he has been obedient to those words of Milton's — which he himself quoted in one of his Poet's Chair addresses — that poetry should be 'simple, serious and passionate'.

The Country Fiddler

My uncle played the fiddle — more elegantly the violin —
A favourite at barn and crossroads dance,
He knew 'The Morning Star' and 'O'Neill's Lament'.

Bachelor head of a house full of sisters,
Runner of poor racehorses, spendthrift,
He left for the New World in an old disgrace.

He left his fiddle in the rafters
When he sailed, never played afterwards,
A rural art stilled in the discord of Brooklyn.

A heavily-built man, tranquil-eyed as an ox,
He ran a wild speakeasy, and died of it.
During the Depression many dossed in his cellar.

I attended his funeral in the Church of the Redemption,
Then, unexpected successor, reversed time
To return where he had been born.

During my schooldays the fiddle rusted
(The bridge fell away, the catgut snapped)
Reduced to a plaything, stinking of stale rosin.

The country people asked if I also had music
(All the family had had) but the fiddle was in pieces
And the rafters remade, before I discovered my craft.

Twenty years afterwards, I saw the church again,
And promised to remember my burly godfather
And his rural craft after this fashion:

So succession passes, through strangest hands.

A Chosen Light (1967)
and *The Rough Field (1972)*

Ciaran Carson *The Country Fiddler*

The first line of the poem announces leitmotifs which will be a preoccupation of its wider context, the acoustic landscape of *The Rough Field*. 'My uncle played the fiddle' — a plain enough statement, but according in its iambic beat to the first bar of a traditional reel. It makes a neat musical contrast to the flowery 'more elegantly the violin', a phrase which we can imagine spoken in a genteel Received Pronunciation. Etymologically, it is probable that both words are from Latin *vitula*, a stringed instrument, from Vitula, the goddess of joy and victory, hence *vitulari*, 'to celebrate joyfully'. The English words have different registers. They are, in a sense, translations of each other; and translation, both in the sense of 'to remove to another place' and 'to render into another language' is at the heart of *The Rough Field*, itself a translation of the place name Garvaghey, *garbh achaidh*, 'a rough field'. *Achaidh* is a Northern variant of *achadh*; and I note that Ó Dónaills's Irish Dictionary cites *Cúig Achadh Uisnigh*, 'the five fields of Uisneach, the five fifths of Ireland'. We think of that iconic Republican song, 'Four Green Fields'. A severed tongue of politics lurks behind the name.

'He knew "The Morning Star" and "O'Neill's Lament"': one tune is a joyous reel, the other not. Later on, the poem entitled 'Lament for the O'Neills' brings the music explicitly into politics, or politics into music, evoking 'burnt houses, pillaged farms, / a province in flames'. We begin to see the fiddle left in the rafters in another light. Traditionally, guns were hidden in the rafters. There is, indeed, a reel known as 'The Gun in the Thatch'; and usually we do not think that fiddles rust, but guns do. In other words, the poem begins to acquire 'the symbolic depth-charge of music', as Montague has it later on in the volume.

If *The Rough Field* can be thought of as a musical composition, it is not so much symphony as fugue — a word which applies both to 'continuously shifting melodic fragments that remain, in the "tune" sense, perpetually unfinished', as Glenn Gould has it, and to an amnesiac state in which the sufferer loses his identity and takes on another. I well remember the impact that Montague's book had on me when it first appeared in 1972. In its ambitious patterning, its *bricolage* of quotations set as marginalia to the poems, its obsessive circling around themes of exile and identity, its concern with language and music, it seemed like a more urgent retelling of *The Waste Land*: modernist in scope and method, but shot through with personal anxiety and grief for the loss of a cultural hinterland.

At the time I was only beginning to write seriously. In the same year I published my first pamphlet, *The Insular Celts*, whose title poem Montague would later include in *The Faber Book of Irish Verse*. In retrospect, I can now acknowledge the influence of *The Rough Field* on other books of mine, most obviously perhaps in *Belfast Confetti*; and more latterly if more obliquely in *For All We Know*, which uses the Glenn Gould quote above as one of its epigraphs.

'So succession passes, through strangest hands.'

A Bright Day

for John McGahern

At times I see it, present
   As a bright day, or a hill,
The only way of saying something
   Luminously as possible.

Not the accumulated richness
   Of an old historical language —
That musk-deep odour!
   But a slow exactness

Which recreates experience
   By ritualizing its details —
Pale web of curtain, width
   Of deal table, till all

Takes on a witch-bright glow
   And even the clock on the mantel
Moves its hands in a fierce delight
   Of so, and so, and so.

A Chosen Light (1967)
and *The Rough Field (1972)*

Seamus Heaney *A Bright Day*

It may be short, and shy of high talk, but 'A Bright Day' is a visionary poem, an undisappointed *Gile na Gile*, what the poet calls elsewhere 'an errant music, / Clear, strange, beautiful'. Since I first read it more than forty years ago I have loved it for its art, at once delicately tentative and utterly sure-footed, but even more for what the art affords, a sense that the veil has trembled, that the glass we see through darkly has been momentarily and uncannily made clear. There are many poems in the Montague *Collected* that are more grievously burdened with matters of great personal and historical import but none that is more the pure lyric thing, 'half-imagined and half-real', given to him and only him to write.

When it was published in *A Chosen Light* (1967) John was already at work on another, very different poem that again only he could write, a payment of dues to lost tradition, informed by *pietas* and pride, by a creative tension between subjectivity and historical witness, between the Yeatsian command to 'lie down where all the ladders start' and the Miloszian question, 'What is poetry that does not save / Nations and peoples?' *The Rough Field* would not appear until 1972, but as he wrote, the poet must have experienced the different fulfilments of bardic and lyric utterance, empowered as he was by memories of the *file* at the inauguration stone and the water-carrying boy-poet at the widening pool. All of which would have strengthened and refined a poetic intelligence already sharply aware of its situation between *mythos* and modernity, in a landscape where at one moment 'the bird of total meaning / stirs upon its hidden branch' and at another the autobiographical speaker concedes 'Our finally lost dream of man at home / in a rural setting'.

In every decade since the late 1950s there have been classic Montague achievements in both registers. Of one group we might say, 'Ireland's history in their lineaments trace'; of another, that they 'Snatch out of time the passionate transitory'; but of none, 'This is better than "A Bright Day"'.

Here the vision is mediated through a window, a wind's

eye between the hill outside and table inside, between the permanent and the immanent; but it is mediated also through the poet's ear, through enjambements that hesitate and pass as ineluctably as the second hand of that clock on the mantel, through rhymes that compound the ritual with the usual, commingle the 'hill' with the 'possible', the 'richness' with the 'exactness', the 'all' with the 'details', the 'so' with the 'glow'. And by the end of the poem that 'witch-bright glow' beyond the curtained pane transmits a weird electric charge into the language. There is magic, we might say, in the molossus; the light that shines in those three stressed syllables is the same as that which shines above the dancers in 'Beyond the Liss' and bathes the scene at the end of 'All Legendary Obstacles' where the *cailleach* marks 'A neat circle on the glass' and peers through an equally bewitching window as the lovers 'Move into the wet darkness / Kissing, still unable to speak'.

Forge

The whole shed smelt of dead iron:
the dented teeth of a harrow,
the feminine pathos of donkeys' shoes.

A labourer backed in a Clydesdale.
Hugely fretful, its nostrils dilated
while the smith viced a hoof

in his apron, wrestling it
to calmness, as he sheared the pith
like wood-chips, to a rough circle.

Then the bellows sang in the tall chimney
waking the sleeping metal, to leap
on the anvil. As I was slowly

beaten to a matching curve
the walls echoed the stress
of the verb *to forge*.

A Chosen Light (1967)

Vona Groarke *Forge*

It's not every poet who can back a Clydesdale into a poem. John Montague not only gets one effortlessly into 'The Forge', he then seems to step just far enough away to allow the horse to draw up into an impressive and marvellous physicality.

As readers, we may walk into his forge behind Montague, but then he stands, as it were, alongside us, so that what the poem shows seems to happen directly in front of us as an unmediated and spontaneous event. The shoeing of the horse is nicely described, with most of the energy invested in those wisely chosen verbs.

John Montague is the consummate observer, always on the lookout for the giveaway detail. So much hinges on 'hugely fretful' with its strategic adverb/adjective combination that conjures up a horse that is bristling and restless, and yet unable to break free into the comparative release of one true verb.

That verb, when it comes in the final line, is manipulated with tremendous force and drama. Now a firm nudge requires us to shift our consideration away from the horse and onto the poet. The nostril-dilated horse and the singing bellows cede to another kind of breath — the life-force of language, the stress and echo of the verb 'to forge'. That the verb is fastened onto the poem's cusp, where it rings with the clarity and authority of the horseshoe itself, indicates a poet who knows how to work the language to achieve the desired effect.

The only forge I ever entered was a one-roomed, half-doored, drystone shed near Furbo in County Galway where my father took me when I was six or so. I have a clear image of it even now, how pools of musk and darkness seemed to stand like silent horses in the corners of the room; how the fire had a kind of personality that made us listen to it and watch its every move. It was an intriguing and yet comforting place with its steady rhythms and unknowable, livid fire. The building is still there, just about, roofless, unlit and long since covered in ivy, with a local hotel's billboard fixed to the Galway side. 'The Forge' brought it back to me; the apron, the bellows, the anvil, the clamour of fire and thrumming work. I had forgotten I remembered it until I read this poem. The 'dead iron' in the opening line isn't long being struck into life by the practised hand of this poet. The 'real' forge, which is every forge (including my own remembered one), becomes an emblematic space where the resonance of language hammers home. That this is achieved with such apparent effortlessness confirms what we already know from so many John Montague poems: that his steady hand wrestles language to calmness, and that his is a dedicated, wise, ample and forceful gift.

Division

i.m. Theodore Roethke

1

There is no hawk among my friends.
Swiftly they cruise their chosen air,
Not to spy the grey fieldmouse
And plummet fiercely to the moor,
But to survey a heaven, inspect
The small, the far. Is it news
That the beetle's back is abstract,
A jewel box; the ash pod has glider wings?
Cruelty is not their way of life,
Nor indifference; they ride the currents
To grasp the invisible. The service
They do shapes also what they are
And the fernlike talon uncurls:
There is no hawk among my friends.

2

There are days when the head is
A bitter, predatory thing
Which will not let oneself
Or others alone, prying, rending!

It is a chill sensuality
Which outdistances cruelty
As though destruction were
A releasing element

Down which the mind patrols —
A wide vanned golden eagle —

Seizing the unnecessary, the small,
With juridical claws.

But sometimes when it sails
Too swift, between the wings' pause,
I know that my own best life
Is the hypnotized fieldmouse

Housed beneath its claws.

A Chosen Light (1967)

David Wheatley *Division*

'There is no hawk among my friends. / Swiftly they cruise their chosen air . . .' The opening lines of John Montague's 'Division' move to an unmistakably Roethkean beat, absorbing the 'Yeats in the speakeasy' quality for which Montague praises the American poet in his memoir *Company*. Fittingly enough for a poem of its title, 'Division' comes in two parts and stakes out an intermediary space, between the human and the avian. There is more than a little ambiguity as the poem's first part develops as to who its 'they' might be. 'Cruelty is not their way of life', Montague writes, and if we are still talking of hawks the raptor-fancier author of 'Hawk Roosting' ('My manners are tearing off heads') might beg to differ; and if of the poet's friends, they end up inconveniently sprouting a 'fernlike talon'. I presume, then, that Montague intends something in between, a man-bird hybrid (the next poem from *A Chosen Light* — in the *Collected Poems* at least — features that archetypal man-bird King Sweeney, and another example, Fintan from *The Book of Invasions*, turns up in a *Mount Eagle* poem, 'Survivor').

The poem's second section takes an inward turn. In 'Night Crow', Roethke felt an avian presence 'Deep in the brain, far back', just as in Beckett's 'The Vulture' the bird drags 'his hunger through the sky / of my skull'. For Montague, 'There are days when the head is / A bitter, predatory thing'. He takes a gamble on his use of abstract nouns ('It is a chill sensuality / Which outdistances cruelty / As though destruction were / A releasing element // Down which the mind patrols') before allowing the poem its solving, scattering resolution:

> *But sometimes when it sails*
> *Too swift, between the wings' pause,*
> *I know that my own best life*
> *Is the hypnotized fieldmouse*
>
> *Housed beneath its claws.*

43

Over half a century and more Montague has explored the theme of division and self-division, speaking through the grafted second tongue of American exile and return. Yet for all the sombreness of self-alienation, civil discord or marital strife, it is obvious that Montague's greatest tests, as subject matter, provide the basis for how his poetry functions at its most exacting, urgent and true. 'Division' articulates a poetics whose speaker is both bird and human, hawk and prey, self and other. As Montague's readers we may hitch a ride on his raptor currents or clutch like fieldmice at the earth, but cannot escape the pull of this many-minded art, serving an elemental need that, like Beckett's vulture, will not come to rest 'till hunger earth and sky be offal'.

The Wild Dog Rose

i.m. Minnie Kearney

1

I go to say goodbye to the cailleach,
that terrible figure who haunted my childhood
but no longer harsh, a human being
merely, hurt by event.
                        The cottage,
circled by trees, weathered to admonitory
shapes of desolation by the mountain winds,
straggles into view. The rank thistles
and leathery bracken of untilled fields
stretch behind with — a final outcrop —
the hooped figure by the roadside,
its retinue of dogs
                        which give tongue
as I approach, with savage, whingeing cries
so that she slowly turns, a moving nest
of shawls and rags, to view, to stare
the stranger down.
                        And I feel again
that ancient awe, the terror of a child
before the great hooked nose, the cheeks
dewlapped with dirt, the staring blue
of the sunken eyes, the mottled claws
clutching a stick
                        but now hold
and return her gaze, to greet her,
as she greets me, in friendliness.
Memories have wrought reconciliation
between us, we talk in ease at last,
like old friends, lovers almost,
sharing secrets
                        of neighbours

she quarrelled with, who now lie
in Garvaghey graveyard, beyond all hatred;
of my family and hers, how she never married,
though a man came asking in her youth.
'You would be loath to leave your own,'
she sighs, 'and go among strangers' —
his parish ten miles off.
                              For sixty years
since, she has lived alone, in one place.
Obscurely honoured by such confidences,
I idle by the summer roadside, listening,
while the monologue falters, continues,
rehearsing the small events of her life.
The only true madness is loneliness,
the monotonous voice in the skull
that never stops
                    because never heard.

2

And there
where the dog rose shines in the hedge
she tells me a story so terrible
that I try to push it away,
my bones melting.
                    Late at night
a drunk came beating at her door
to break it in, the bolt snapping
from the soft wood, the thin mongrels
rushing to cut, but yelping as
he whirls with his farm boots
to crush their skulls.
                    In the darkness
they wrestle, two creatures crazed

with loneliness, the smell of the
decaying cottage in his nostrils
like a drug, his body heavy on hers,
the tasteless trunk of a seventy-year-
old virgin, which he rummages while
she battles for life
                              bony fingers
reaching desperately to push
against his bull neck. 'I prayed
to the Blessed Virgin herself
for help and after a time
I broke his grip.'
                              He rolls
to the floor, snores asleep,
while she cowers until dawn
and the dogs' whimpering starts
him awake, to lurch back across
the wet bog.

   3

                              And still
the dog rose shines in the hedge.
Petals beaten wide by rain, it
sways slightly, at the tip of a
slender, tangled, arching branch
which, with her stick, she gathers
into us.
              'The wild rose
is the only rose without thorns,'
she says, holding a wet blossom
for a second, in a hand knotted
as the knob of her stick.
'Whenever I see it, I remember

the Holy Mother of God and
all she suffered.'
                    Briefly
the air is strong with the smell
of that weak flower, offering
its crumbling yellow cup
and pale bleeding lips
fading to white
                    at the rim
of each bruised and heart-
shaped petal.

Tides (1970)
and *The Rough Field (1972)*

John McAuliffe *The Wild Dog Rose*

In 1991 I spent a fortnight at the Yeats Summer School, a prize for a Writers' Week competition. I didn't know what to expect. Beforehand I re-read the Red Hanrahan poems, with occasional glances forward to Crazy Jane. I wasn't disappointed when I met Sligo's gathering of American and European Yeatsians who ran séances when the pubs shut and seemed minded to believe in fairies.

Every morning, though, I would struggle up from the youth hostel to Brian John's class on Thomas Kinsella and John Montague, poets I'd read carefully that year in Galway. The poem that most caught my attention then was 'The Wild Dog Rose'. Its story and images could not have been further from the summer school's carefree night-time activities, although it too was informed differently by Yeats's example, by that sense of responsibility and public address which drives the book in which it found its home, *The Rough Field*.

It is a big poem and combines many different elements of Irish poetry: it begins with the *cailleach*, and a sense of that national tradition, that 'heavy greenness' with which Montague has always engaged. He has argued with that tradition from the start, and here he refuses the usual images associated with the hag, stage-managing instead the realistic coming-to-life of that archetype in the poet's old neighbour. But the poem is not just a note on earlier literature. Its strong narrative leads its readers into images of violence and sex which are still shocking now, 'Leda and the Swan' filtered into *The Great Hunger*, the verbs brutally effective as the neighbour 'rummages' the old woman's body.

But the poem is more than an indictment of Dev's Ireland and when it breaks off meditatively, 'The only true madness is loneliness, / the monotonous voice in the skull / that never stops', it lights up the woman's character from a larger, human perspective. And how do we read the complicated irony of her protest: 'I prayed / to the Blessed Virgin herself / for help and after a time / broke his grip'?

The poem avoids any predictable or party finish, and closes

instead with the delicately sexual, loving and musical description of the dog rose, 'at the tip of a / slender, tangled, arching branch', 'that weak flower' with which the poem aims to restore the woman, as it also extends to its readers a greater sense of what an Irish poem could do.

Life Class

The infinite softness
& complexity of a body
in repose. The hinge

of the ankle bone de-
fines the flat space
of a foot, its puckered

flesh & almost arch.
The calf's heavy curve
sweeping down against

the bony shin, or up
to the warm bulges and
hollows of the knee

describes a line of
gravity, energy as
from shoulder knob

to knuckle, the arm
cascades, round the
elbow, over the wrist.

The whole body a system
of checks & balances —
those natural shapes

a sculptor celebrates,
sea-worn caves, pools,
boulders, tree-trunks —

        or, at every hand's turn,
        a crop of temptation:
        arm & thigh opening

on softer, more secret
areas, hair sprouting
crevices, odorous nooks

& crannies of love,
awaiting the impress
of desire, a fervent

homage, or tempting
to an extinction of
burrowing blindness.

(Deviously uncurling
from the hot clothes
of shame, a desert

father's dream of
sluttish nakedness,
demon with inflamed

breasts, dangling
tresses to drag man
down to hell's gaping

vaginal mouth.)

> To see the model
> as simply human
>
> a mild housewife
> earning pocket money
> for husband, child,
>
> is to feel the dark
> centuries peel away
> to the innocence of

the white track on
her shoulders where
above brown flesh

the brassiere lifts
to show the quiet of
unsunned breasts &

to mourn & cherish
each melancholy proof
of mortality's grudge

against perfection:
the appendix scar
lacing the stomach

the pale stitches on
the wailing wall of
the rib-cage where

the heart obediently
pumps.

What homage
is worthy for such

a gentle unveiling?
To nibble her ten
toes, in an ecstacy

of love, to drink
hair, like water?
(Fashion designers

would flatten her
breasts, level the
curves of arse &

        stomach, moulding
        the mother lode
        that pulses beneath

        to a uniformity
        of robot bliss.)

On cartridge paper

an army of pencils
deploy silently to
lure her into their

net of lines while
from & above her
chilled, cramped

body blossoms
a late flower:
her tired smile.

Tides (1970)

Medbh McGuckian *Life Class*

I bought a second-hand copy of *Tides* as an undergraduate, more for its physical beauty than any full comprehension, never dreaming I might one day meet its author. Knowing little of my own tides, or the mystery of being a woman, I found this poem among others there fascinating, informative, sensitive to the female viewpoint. I had no idea how to write about being a woman or relating to one. It seemed a daring outspokenness for an Irish Catholic voice then, a step beyond Kavanagh, more in the realistic vein of McGahern or Moore, more sympathetic than Joyce. Dated in a way now, I still find the broken verse form encapsulating twin opposed attitudes to the feminine body tender, sensuous, brutal and passionate, as Montague so often is in his wide range of exquisite love poems.

I once attended a poetry reading by Seamus Heaney where he came under attack for having the women in his poems 'always up to their oxters in flour'. While this could not be levelled at Montague, his women, for they are numerous, tend rather to be spreadeagled in hotel bedrooms, though more romantically than Muldoon's. In this longish meditation, the woman is isolated, a nude model, subject to the phallic gaze and penetration of 'an army of pencils'. She is also a bait or fish-quarry, a favourite trope of Montague's, to be goaded into the net of the drawings and equally of the poem itself. Her body, as so frequently in his poetry, is compared to the natural world of plants of which her forced smile is the blossom.

I believe that something of this poem must have entered the title poem of my own first volume, *The Flower Master*, and indeed the title poem of *Drawing Ballerinas*. The first section of the poem could apply to a male body as much as a female, although there is a softness and grace that suggest the feminine. Everything is safely under the control of the eye and mind until without warning, as the imagery takes off into caves and pools, the sexual arousal of the viewer warms to the possibility that this exposed nakedness is a harvest actually available. He uses the word 'love' as a synonym for sex, then in brackets describes the guilty lust and sin-obsessed wrestlings of a Hopkins or mediaeval scribe.

The tides of the poem then revert, as after orgasm, to a repeat of the initial calm contemplation, pondering the internal mental state of the paid worker, her acceptance and financial necessity. Here her body is discussed more intimately as if, from within the woman herself, the poet succeeds in entering the living reality of the female body with its history of suffering, its scars and stitches, a highly unusual capacity for empathy that Montague demonstrates elsewhere. There is a more physiological emphasis here which acknowledges the ever-threatening presence of death.

The mood darkens once again to a rhetorical questioning of the morality of looking at a woman in this way, where she becomes food and drink like a Eucharist. He criticizes the negative effect of modern dress reshaping and denying the fertility of the traditional womb, reducing women to mechanical clones of themselves. There seems to me a rural self-consciousness here in his juxtaposition of the words 'brassiere' and 'arse', not used satirically but perfectly seriously. He sails close to the shore of political offensiveness for a contemporary audience, were it not for the immediate follow-up of reverence given to 'the mother lode'. Montague's poems are among the most lucid and honest in their praise and appraisal of women, because of his deep and total appreciation of his mother, his strange upbringing which he details so accurately.

This is an achievement of self-scrutiny as much as of voyeurism. The passive muse triumphs spiritually over the freezing paralysis of her stark circumstances to resist final or total capture by anyone. The pun in 'tired' hints that she manages to protect and even to clothe herself 'as when in silks my Julia goes' in defiance of exhaustion. Despite its old-fashioned air, this particular poem remains for me a life class, teaching the sadness and economy of what might still be called the flesh.

'Hearing the cock crow in the dark . . .'

Hearing the cock crow in the dark,
The first thing to move in the desolate farmyard,
I lay awake to listen, the tripled shrill calls
As jagged and chill as water
While a pale movement of dawn
Began to climb and outline
The dark window-frame.

Those were my first mornings,
Fresh as Eden, with dew on the face,
Like first kiss, the damp air:
On dismantled flagstones,
From ash-smoored embers
Hands now strive to rekindle
That once leaping fire.

The Rough Field (1972)

Thomas Kinsella *'Hearing the cock crow in the dark . . .'*

I have chosen these lines from among many for their clear manifestation of the unique quality of John's best verse: delicacy grounded on strength — a strength often unrecognized by the unwary.

A Lost Tradition

All around, shards of a lost tradition:
From the Rough Field I went to school
In the Glen of the Hazels. Close by
Was the bishopric of the Golden Stone;
The cairn of Carleton's homesick poem.

Scattered over the hills, tribal-
And placenames, uncultivated pearls.
No rock or ruin, *dún* or dolmen
But showed memory defying cruelty
Through an image-encrusted name.

The heathery gap where the Rapparee,
Shane Barnagh, saw his brother die —
On a summer's day the dying sun
Stained its colours to crimson:
So breaks the heart, Brish-mo-Cree.

The whole landscape a manuscript
We had lost the skill to read,
A part of our past disinherited;
But fumbled, like a blind man,
Along the fingertips of instinct.

The last Gaelic speaker in the parish
When I stammered my school Irish
One Sunday after mass, crinkled
A rusty litany of praise:
Tá an Ghaeilge againn arís . . . *

Tír Eoghain: Land of Owen,
Province of the O'Niall;
The ghostly tread of O'Hagan's
Barefoot gallowglasses marching
To merge forces in Dún Geannainn

Push southward to Kinsale!
Loudly the war-cry is swallowed
In swirls of black rain and fog
As Ulster's pride, Elizabeth's foemen,
Founder in a Munster bog.

The Rough Field (1972)

We have the Irish again.

Eavan Boland *A Lost Tradition*

I remember exactly where I was when I first read 'All Legendary Obstacles'. It was my introduction to John Montague's work and it was 1966. The big, awkward-to-hold Dolmen book, with its cream endpapers and mock-vellum boards was a true surprise.

It was also the year of my final exams at Trinity. I would be required therefore, for hour upon hour, to answer questions on British court poets and Renaissance essayists. Now here, all of a sudden, was an Irish poet, as familiar with the Central Valley as Garvaghey, inscribing both with a migrant, unsettled and luminously estranged sense of place.

For all that, it would take time before I understood the full force of that perspective. With the publication of *The Rough Field* in 1972 it became much clearer. Many poets have a lyric sense of place; some have a narrative bent for displacement. But with the strategies in *The Rough Field*, John Montague dashes the two together, subverting the melody of belonging with the squawk of dispossession. It seemed to me then, and does now, that the poems here are particularly scalding when the plainspoken, powerless world of the individual meets an equally dispossessed history. And so it is in the beautiful piece, 'A Lost Tradition'.

'The whole landscape a manuscript / We had lost the skill to read.' These eloquent lines, coming as they do at the start of the fourth stanza, follow hard on a catalogue of iconic memories and memorable losses: the heathery gap where a Rapparee saw his brother die, the bishopric which Carleton signalled to. This is, again, the alloy of narrative and lyric, but the sweep is ambitious and impressive in a way which that alloy often fails to be. As the poem unfolds, the landscape gives up its meaning, and the reader is drawn into it:

> *A part of our past disinherited,*
> *But fumbled, like a blind man,*
> *Along the fingertips of instinct.*

'A Lost Tradition' is not a comfortable poem. I still think that today as I re-read its account of failures and defeats. The schoolboy at the start, who went to school from the rough field to the Glen of the Hazels, who stammers his 'school Irish' in the middle of the poem to 'the last Gaelic speaker in the parish', has become the poet at the end of the piece, fitting these losses and generations together, making a bleak inventory of what cannot be retrieved. And thereby, of course, retrieving it.

History as failure. Language as recovery. There is something deeply moving about the unswerving account of the first here, and the subtle inference of the second. 'A Lost Tradition' seems to me an important poem in John Montague's work, and an utterly essential one in the Irish poetic tradition. It writes down who we are and have been. As well as where and why. No small feat for any poem. When Yeats wrote his preface to a book of short stories at the end of the nineteenth century, he wrote of those storytellers that they 'tried to make one see life plainly, but all written down in a kind of fiery shorthand'. And so it is here. And so it will remain.

Seskilgreen

A circle of stones
surviving behind a
guttery farmhouse,

the capstone phallic
in a thistly meadow:
Seskilgreen Passage Grave.

Cup, circle,
triangle beating
their secret dance

(eyes, breasts,
thighs of a still
fragrant goddess).

I came last in May
to find the mound
drowned in bluebells

with a fearless wren
hoarding speckled eggs
in a stony crevice

while cattle
swayed sleepily
under low branches

lashing the ropes
of their tails
across the centuries.

A Slow Dance (1975)

Peter Fallon *Seskilgreen*

Surely it's not because Seskilgreen (like its neighbouring Knockmany whose 'brooding tumulus' also features in poems by John Montague) is aligned to the noonday sun *and* to Loughcrew that I've admired and treasured this poem since I read it first more than thirty years ago. It's not. That fact might have drawn me to it but it hasn't justified my liking for it.

'Seskilgreen' is one of a number of poems in which this meticulous anatomist, bard, score-keeper, even an Odysseus of Ulster, reads the contours of the landscape as if they were Braille. Like the pilgrim to the Penal Rock at Altamuskin he 'learns the massrock's lesson'. The poem appeared first in *A Slow Dance* as Part IV of the title sequence, a sequence which discloses an intimacy with the earth and which includes also 'For the Hillmother', one of Montague's incantatory, pagan prayers, or 'blessings'.

It is a poem of uncommon economy — eight stanzas with a mere three, short, unrhymed lines in each. No line comprises more than six syllables. (One counts them so carefully because they're so scarce.) It differs from other short-lined poems in *A Small Dance* and other collections, poems such as 'Small Secrets', 'Mother Cat' and 'A Courtyard in Queens' (or 'What a View', 'Special Delivery' and 'Life Class') in that those poems unfold and relax in the meandering progression of their narratives and descriptions.

'Seskilgreen' begins with field notes, two patterns of six-line records, the first of them a run of calligraphic brush-strokes that animates a clearly familiar scene, with its neatly fitting, natural and convincing local tones ('guttery', 'thistly'). These lines preface the three capitalized nouns that follow the colon and amplify the poem's short title. They serve as a herald to line 6, whose bold announcement contains an air of discovery and the force of revelation.

The second six lines are further distilled: two of them with only two words in each, and these both nouns ('Cup, circle' . . . 'eyes, breasts') that stand unmodified, unadorned, unencumbered. Staccato. They are given their own space which, in turn, they earn by their command of it.

These four stanzas, a unit of introduction, pave the way for the line in the poem with the most words in it, a line which foregrounds the author, or observer, and records both the recent past and his most recent visit. By registering a season of fecund growth ('drowned in bluebells') and renewal (that brave incubator!), it asserts the persistence of an ancient world.

'Seskilgreen' addresses and answers a question posed in *The Rough Field*: what remains permanently? The cattle in this poem aren't the abattoir-bound stores, that 'clump of bullocks' of 'The Source' that 'gaze at me . . . turning their slow surprise / Upon their tongue', all of which exist and breathe in a present moment. Steadfast, obdurate, the cattle in 'Seskilgreen' flagellate constant ages.

In several poems (the address to a 'Harsh landscape that haunts me' appears in two of them, before its famous acknowledgement of 'all my circling a failure to return') John Montague concedes to change and admits what is 'gone'. In 'Seskilgreen', from 'circle' (the opening noun, alliterating across the span of all twenty-four lines) to 'centuries' (the closing, part-anagrammatic noun) he fixes time and its cycles. The poem exemplifies the mastery of one fluent in the art of seeing and saying. In few more than a hundred syllables it encompasses a site and subject that is actual and yet borders on the mythical.

This poem is a triumph of synergy.

Courtyard in Winter

Snow curls in on the cold wind.

Slowly, I push back the door.
After long absence, old habits
Are painfully revived, those disciplines
Which enable us to survive,
To keep a minimal fury alive
While flake by faltering flake

Snow curls in on the cold wind.

Along the courtyard, the boss
Of each cobblestone is rimmed
In white, with winter's weight
Pressing, like a silver shield,
On all the small plots of earth,
Inert in their living death as

Snow curls in on the cold wind.

Seized in a giant fist of frost,
The grounded planes at London Airport,
Mallarmé swans, trapped in ice.
The friend whom I have just left
Will be dead, a year from now,
Through her own fault, while

Snow curls in on the cold wind.

Or smothered by some glacial truth?
Thirty years ago, I learnt to reach
Across the rusting hoops of steel
That bound our greening waterbarrel
To save the living water beneath
The hardening crust of ice, before

Snow curls in on the cold wind.

But despair has a deeper crust.
In all our hours together, I never
Managed to ease the single hurt
That edged her towards her death;
Never reached through her loneliness
To save a trust, chilled after

Snow curls in on the cold wind.

I plunged through snowdrifts once,
Above our home, to carry
A telegram to a mountain farm.
Fearful but inviting, they waved me
To warm myself at the flaring
Hearth before I faced again where

Snow curls in on the cold wind.

The news I brought was sadness.
In a far city, someone of their name
Lay dying. The tracks of foxes,
Wild birds, as I climbed down
Seemed to form a secret writing
Minute and frail as life when

Snow curls in on the cold wind.

Sometimes, I know that message.
There is a disease called snow-sickness;
The glare from the bright god,
The earth's reply. As if that
Ceaseless, glittering light was
All the truth we'd left after

Snow curls in on the cold wind.

So, before dawn, comfort fails.
I imagine her end, in some sad
Bedsitting room, the steady hiss
Of the gas more welcome than an
Act of friendship, the protective
Oblivion of a lover's caress if

Snow curls in on the cold wind.

In the canyon of the street
The dark snowclouds hesitate,
Turning to slush almost before
They cross the taut canvas of
The street stalls, the bustle
Of a sweeper's brush after

Snow curls in on the cold wind.

The walls are spectral, white.
All the trees black-ribbed, bare.
Only veins of ivy, the sturdy
Laurel with its waxen leaves,
Its scant red berries, survive
To form a winter wreath as

Snow curls in on the cold wind.

What solace but endurance, kindness?
Against her choice, I still affirm
That nothing dies, that even from
Such bitter failure memory grows;
The snowflake's structure, fragile
But intricate as the rose when

Snow curls in on the cold wind.
A Slow Dance (1975)

Seán Lysaght *Courtyard in Winter*

'Courtyard in Winter' appeared in *A Slow Dance*, a book I bought on its publication in 1975, when I was a first-year student at UCC. Montague's presence in Cork at that time, among others such as Seán Lucy and Thomas McCarthy, brought the *actualité* of Irish poetry within my reach. The slim new volume from Dolmen/Oxford was proof of the connection between my new locality and the wider world of reputation and approval. (At eighteen I was too unsure of myself to become one of the regulars at Montague's house, but I did visit once, escorted by Tom McCarthy, the first person I met who had a serious commitment to the craft of poetry.)

The occasion of the poem is a suicide, a lonely denial of so many of the relationships that connect people through trust, sharing and good faith. It also stands full square against the hope with which poetry is made. To attempt to write poetry in response to suicide is to send a probe into a black hole where it may be swallowed before it has any opportunity of sending back a reliable record.

As the writer sets out on this mission in 'Courtyard in Winter', he clearly does so with a redemptive purpose, but he is also aware of the challenge he faces. The stakes are high, so the poem begins tentatively, with only a minimal observation, which becomes a refrain: '*Snow curls in on the cold wind.*' 'Slowly,' he writes in terms of cautious self-scrutiny, 'I push back the door': the question is whether the act of writing will be adequate to its subject. Although the writer has at his disposal the archetypes of literary tradition and their rhetorical apparatus, the first stanza delays these until line 5, when a Yeatsian 'minimal fury' is delivered at the same time as the rhyme 'alive' to close the couplet. Then, with the adoption of the refrain — another Yeatsian trope — it is clear that literary form is here determined to make a stand.

The second stanza evokes the stark, elemental struggle of life through the winter with the antiquarian motif of the shield pressing down on a dormant earth. We are then catapulted forward to a modern winter where, on the rebound, the poet plays with time, turning his final farewell with the dead friend into a present tense: 'The friend whom I have just left / Will be dead, a year from now.'

If some of the devices suggest a debt to Yeats, the under-currents here are Wordsworthian: memories of his native countryside come to assist him as he demonstrates the endurance of life through bleak conditions. There's a wonderful, life-affirming exuberance in 'I plunged through snowdrifts once', breaking through the solemnity of the piece like the play of children at a wake. The 'flaring / Hearth' of the mountain farm where he delivered the news of a dying relative has the intensity of *Wuthering Heights*, another theatre of survival in harsh circumstances. On his way back, animal tracks in the snow have the mysterious potency of hieroglyphs; their 'Minute and frail' characters also operate typographically, as black marks on the white page.

All these affirmations turn on the axis of the poem's central disclosure in the ninth stanza: 'So, before dawn, comfort fails.' At its bleakest moment, however, even here, literacy pulls language back from the brink: the Beckettian touch is unmistakable, as Montague anticipates by several years the searing poignancy of *Ohio Impromptu*; the details of the suicide during a hard London winter reverberate inevitably to Plath. These associations, I believe, crystallize around the poem and strengthen it.

In the second- and third-last stanzas, the poet attempts a recovery with reference to an outside world to get away from the tragic confinement of the 'sad / Bedsitting room'. The eye of the solitary writer is on the weather, but still captures in passing the street stalls and the street sweepers, images of ordinary life carrying on through the dark months.

With the end in sight, the writer's instincts lead him to look for figurative and symbolic elements: the survey of trees and foliage is distilled into the 'winter wreath' of the laurel. Here the classical symbol of victory and artistic excellence is attenuated to a memorial tribute, but the sense of a contest is still strong. And finally, as he makes his calm assertion of life and its enduring memories, the poem transforms the snowflake itself into a symbol, 'fragile/ But intricate as the rose'.

This substantial poem confronts a bleak moment without false rhetoric and even without feigned modesty. A poet in impressive command of tradition manages to pick his way through the debris of memory and association to get to the site of a tragedy. From this position of absolute desolation, where 'comfort fails', he recovers a measure of faith in life's process.

Windharp

for Patrick Collins

The sounds of Ireland,
that restless whispering
you never get away
from, seeping out of
low bushes and grass,
heatherbells and fern,
wrinkling bog pools,
scraping tree branches,
light hunting cloud,
sound hounding sight,
a hand ceaselessly
combing and stroking
the landscape, till
the valley gleams
like the pile upon
a mountain pony's coat.

A Slow Dance (1975)

Michael Longley *Windharp*

I have loved 'Windharp' for a long time. It was love at first sight. The narrow shape on the page helps to create this poem's strange effulgence — as a single shaft of sunlight breaking through on an overcast day focuses our attention on features in the landscape — a searchlight. Many of John Montague's finest poems deploy short lines and need to be read aloud with a nano-second's pause at the end of each line. This applies even (or perhaps especially) when the lines end with apparently unimportant words such as 'of' and 'till'. For instance, in its fourth line ('from, seeping out of') the poem finds its balance precisely. Syllable and breathing-space interact with great refinement. We read these lines with bated breath and are drawn into an enraptured state of mind. Attentive, devout even, 'Windharp' is a halting prayer, a broken spell. We are carried away and then brought down to earth.

I look up to this celebrant of the Irish countryside, the precision of his descriptions. The spare music, cool as a breeze, lifts the 'heatherbells and fern' and the 'bog pools' well away from the stereotypical. Spaced in the single sentence like rosary beads on their thread the participles — 'whispering', 'wrinkling', 'stroking' — generate an atmosphere of suspense. Adverbs can so often be superfluous but here the solitary adverb 'ceaselessly' is detonated brilliantly and in a way becomes the soul of the poem. Its sounds are what these sixteen lines are all about. The intensity of 'Windharp' lends its particulars an emblematic aura. One concise rural evocation comes to symbolize the whole island. Implicated in every detail, the poet's love of Ireland is most beautifully embodied in the heart-stopping final image of the mountain pony, an incarnation of the spirit of the countryside, the poet's Pegasus.

I am reminded of when I first met John Montague decades ago on the campus of Queen's University in Belfast. He emerged out of the darkness of the quadrangle and into the dimly lit colonnade that led to the lecture theatre where he was going to read. This poet whom I had been studying for years all of a sudden took shape like one of his slim-lined poems. 'We meet at last,' he said. He was nimble and wry, a commanding presence, and friendlier than he needed to be. He read very well, with the audience gradually growing accustomed to his unpredictable stammer. The literary conversation that followed was full of angles like a good game of squash. And so it continues. I want to wish this complicated man and superlative poet a happy 80th birthday. It is high time I thanked him for his poems and for his devotion to the craft, 'a hand ceaselessly / combing and stroking / the landscape'.

A Graveyard in Queens

for Eileen Carney

We hesitate along
flower-encumbered

avenues of the dead;
Greek, Puerto-Rican,

Italian, Irish —
(our true Catholic

world, a graveyard)
but a squirrel

dances us to it
through the water

sprinklered grass,
collapsing wreaths,

& taller than you
by half, lately from

that hidden village
where you were born

I sway with you
in a sad, awkward

dance of pain
over the grave of

my uncle & namesake —
the country fiddler —

& the grave of almost
all your life held,

your husband & son
all three sheltering

under the same
squat, grey stone.

You would cry out
against what has

happened, such
heedless hurt,

had you the harsh
nature for it

(swelling the North
wind with groans,

curses, imprecations
against heaven's will)

but your mind is
a humble house, a

soft light burning
beneath the holy

picture, the image
of the seven times

wounded heart of
her, whose portion

It sent me down
to the millstream

is to endure. For
there is no end

to spy upon a
mournful waterhen

to pain, nor of
love to match it

shushing her young
along the autumn

& I remember Anne
meekest of my aunts

flood, as seriously
as a policeman and

rocking and praying
in her empty room.

after scampering
along, the proud

Oh, the absurdity
of grief in that

plumed squirrel
now halts, to stand

doll's house, all
the chair legs sawn

at the border
of this grave plot

to nurse dead children:
love's museum!

serious, still,
a small ornament

⚬

holding something,
a nut, a leaf —

like an offering
inside its paws.

For an instant
you smile to see

his antics, then
bend to tidy

flowers, gravel,
like any woman

making a bed,
arranging a room,

over what were
your darlings' heads

and far from
our supposed home

I submit again
to stare soberly

at my own name
cut on a gravestone

& hear the creak
of a ghostly fiddle

filter through
American earth

the slow pride
of a lament.

A Slow Dance (1975)

Ciaran Berry on *A Graveyard in Queens*

If you look at New York City on a map you will see, among the markings that delineate streets and rivers, bridges and peninsulas, large swathes of green space that signify, not just the presence of the city's many parks, but also its umpteen graveyards. In the Bronx there's Woodlawn, which occupies more than 400 acres, and where the most notable occupants include Miles Davis and Herman Melville. In Brooklyn there's Greenwood with its ornate Civil War era gates where feral monk parrots make their home. You'll notice, though, as you bend over your map, that most of New York's graveyards are in Queens.

There's a simple reason for this. As the population of Manhattan began to swell in the early nineteenth-century, the dead were uprooted to make room for the living, new tenements built where the deceased had been interred. Today there are more than five million of the departed at rest, or still restless, in the twenty-nine or so graveyards of Queens, where the dead outnumber the living by three to one. On the stone slab over one of those graves is written the name of Louis Armstrong. On another you will find the name of Emma Lazarus whose poem adorns the Statue of Liberty. You will also find, if you look hard enough, a stone inscribed with the name John Montague.

Thankfully for us, it is not the John Montague born in St Catharine's Hospital on Bushwick Avenue, Brooklyn, on February 28th, 1929, the third son of James Montague and Mary ('Molly') Carney. It is instead the poet's uncle and 'namesake', 'the country fiddler' whose grave, which lies in the same plot as those of a second uncle and a cousin, Montague stands over with his still grieving aunt in 'A Graveyard in Queens'.

I'd just arrived in New York when I first came across this poem in a selected volume I found in one of those dusty bookshops that used to dot Manhattan. I felt immediate kinship with the piece's solemn, slightly disoriented poet, who has just returned from the 'hidden village' of his ancestors to this 'American earth', the strange land of his birth. With great pleasure I followed the poet as he is led by a squirrel 'through the water / sprinklered grass' to 'sway' with his aunt above those graves. I could hear, as I can still, their footsteps rising and falling in the many terse, double and triple stressed lines of a piece that sways back and forth between worlds in 'the slow pride / of a lament'.

So effortlessly we're moved here from the poet's present in a graveyard in Queens to his past in that 'doll's house' of aunts in his 'supposed home'. We're even invited to look with him into the future as he submits 'again / to stare soberly' at his 'own name / cut on a gravestone'. Here, and elsewhere, the poem seems to manage shifts not just in time and place, but also in terms of the various meanings the word 'home' might have, not just as dwelling and native land, but also as the abiding place of the affections (which the poet's aunt finds in the grave that holds almost all her life) and as one's abode after death.

Effortlessly too we're led between the earth that holds this particular aunt's 'husband & son' to the air where the 'ghostly fiddle' of that other uncle still creaks, and from the sphere of humans, living and dead, to the sphere of creatures — that squirrel finally coming to a stop holding a nut or leaf 'like an offering / inside its paws' and a waterhen 'mournful' as she shushes her young 'along the autumn // flood', both of which, in this new world of 'collapsing wreaths', offer the poet consolation, just as his presence seems to offer consolation to his widowed aunt.

It seems that all this back and forth is brought about, or at least made more acute and therefore more palpable, by the poet's own displacement, the disorientation of arriving in what seems to be again a new city, a new country, and of finding himself standing on the border between the living and the dead, Ireland and America, the world of adulthood and the world of childhood. Because, as he moves in these couplets, it seems to me the poet too is playing cartographer, orienting himself, and us, by making a map that traces lines between those places and times — a map that offers to guide us a little through a world, a life where there is 'no end // to pain', but also, he would add, 'nor of / love to match it', which is a handy map to have wherever you are.

Ó Riada's Farewell

To have gathered from the air a live tradition.

— Ezra Pound

Roving, unsatisfied ghost,
old friend, lean closer;
leave us your skills:
lie still in the quiet
of your chosen earth.

1

Woodtown Manor, Again

We vigil by the dying fire,
talk stilled for once,
foil clash of rivalry,
fierce Samurai pretence.

Outside a rustle of bramble,
jack fox around the framing
elegance of a friend's house
we both choose to love:

two natives warming ourselves
at the revived fire
in a high-ceilinged room
worthy of Carolan —

clatter of harpsichord
the music leaping
like a long candle flame
to light ancestral faces

pride of music
pride of race

2

Abruptly, closer to self-revelation
than I have ever seen, you speak;
bubbles of unhappiness breaking
the bright surface of 'Till Eulenspiegel'.

'I am in great danger,' you whisper,
as much to the failing fire
as to your friend & listener;
'though, you have great luck'.

Our roles reversed, myself cast
as the light-fingered master,
the lucky dancer on thin ice,
rope walker on his precipice.

3

I sense the magisterial strain
behind your jay's laugh,
ruddy moustached, smiling,
your sharp player's mask.

Instinct wrung and run
awry all day, powers idled
to self-defeat, the vacuum
behind the catalyst's gift.

Beyond the flourish
of personality, peacock
pride of music or language:
a constant, piercing torment!

Signs earlier, a stranger
made to stumble at a bar door,
fatal confusion of the powers
of the upper and lower air.

A playing with fire, leading
you, finally, tempting you
to a malevolence, the
calling of death for another.

4

A door opens,
and she steps into the room,
smothered in a black gown,
harsh black hair falling to her knees,
a pallid tearstained face.

How pretty you look,
Miss Death!

5

Samhain

Sing a song
for the mistress
of the bones

the player
on the black keys
the darker harmonies

light jig
of shoe buckles
on a coffin lid

～

Harsh glint
of the wrecker's lantern
on a jagged cliff

across the ceaseless
glitter of the spume:
a seagull's creak.

The damp-haired
seaweed-stained sorceress
marshlight of defeat

～

Chill of winter
a slowly failing fire
faltering desire

Darkness of Darkness
we meet on our way
in loneliness

Blind Carolan
Blind Raftery
Blind Tadhg

6

Hell Fire Club

Around the house all night
dark music of the underworld,
hyena howl of the unsatisfied,
latch creak, shutter sigh,
the groan and lash of trees,
a cloud upon the moon.

Released demons moan.
A monstrous black tom
couchant on the roofbeam.
The widowed peacock screams
knowing the fox's tooth:
a cry, like rending silk,

& a smell of carrion where
baulked of their prey,
from pane to tall window
pane, they flit, howling
to where he lies, who has
called them from defeat.

Now, their luckless meat,
turning a white pillowed room,
smooth as a bridal suite
into a hospital bed where
a lucid beast fights against
a blithely summoned doom.

At the eye of the storm
a central calm, where
tearstained, a girl child

sleeps cradled in my arms
till the morning points
and you are gone.

7

The Two Gifts

And a nation mourns:
The blind horseman with his harp-carrying servant,
Hurrying through darkness to a great house
Where a lordly welcome waits, as here:
Fingernail spikes in candlelight recall
A ripple & rush of upland streams,
The slant of rain on void eye sockets,
The shrill of snipe over mountains
Where a few stragglers nest in bracken —
After Kinsale, after Limerick, after Aughrim,
After another defeat, to be redeemed
By the curlew sorrow of an aisling.

The little Black Rose
(To be sprinkled with tears)
The Silk of the Kine
(To be shipped as dead meat)

'They tore out my tongue
So I grew another one,'
I heard a severed head
Sing down a bloody stream.

But a lonelier lady mourns,
the muse of a man's particular gift,
Mozart's impossible marriage of fire & ice,

skull sweetness of the last quartets,
Mahler's horn wakening the autumn forest,
the harsh blood pulse of Stravinsky,
the hammer of Boulez
                    which you will never lift.

Never to be named with your peers,
'I am in great danger,' he said;
firecastles of flame,
a name extinguished.

8

Lament

With no family
& no country

a voice rises
out of the threatened beat
of the heart & the brain cells

(not for the broken people
nor for the blood soaked earth)

a voice
like an animal howling
to itself on a hillside
in the empty church of the world

a lament so total
it mourns no one
but the globe itself
turning in the endless halls

of space, populated
with passionless stars

and that always raised voice

(1972-1974)

A Slow Dance (1975)

Michael Coady *Ó Riada's Farewell*

Montague's sequence of eight poems was written in the dark aftermath of the composer Seán Ó Riada's death, aged forty, on the 3rd of October 1971, and the traumatic Bloody Sunday killings of the following January in Derry.

One Sunday morning in the preceding July I had met Ó Riada in Cúil Aodha, where he directed his own beautifully ethnic setting of the community Mass (one of his finest legacies). Afterwards, at the house, Ruth had a welcoming table and the children, prattling in Irish, romped with an Irish wolfhound in and out and around the garden. Musicians, including John Kelly the Clare fiddler and concertina player, struck up. Ó Riada was his charismatic self, with beverages, including poteen, liberally on offer.

On that summer morning of open house in Cúil Aodha, who could have believed that he would be dead by the autumn? Coming in early October, that was like the going down of a chieftain, with fell death suddenly thrusting the teenage Peadar Ó Riada into his father's place at the organ for the funeral. On the national news the burial procession resembled Greek tragedy: the throng of mourners, local and national; Ruth, veiled in black (and soon to follow after) with the cluster of small children; Seán Clárach Mac Domhnaill's Jacobite anthem 'Mo Ghile Mear' chanted in the deep-grained timbre of Cúil Aodha voices, and the fiddler John Kelly's comment by the graveside: *He lifted us all up*.

John Montague was amongst those shouldering the coffin. Like other poets, including Kinsella, Heaney and Seán Lucy, he would commemorate the composer, of whom he has recently written: 'few men have had as direct an effect on my life . . .' Their friendship included the occasional locking of antlers. Ó Riada, with a touch of arrogance and a quasi-aristocratic style to match, was a volatile man of brilliant talents — composer, writer and film-maker, performer, broadcaster, cultural visionary and crusader — his iconoclastic lance always at an extreme angle. Though emotionally wounded in childhood, Montague was, and is, a more measured and urbane man, with a self-preserving instinct for the middle way, better fitted for the long haul. Ó Riada's sensibility included a streak of fatalism, borne out by death at forty, and that preceded by the fear that his creative gift seemed to have run dry.

That compounded pall overhangs 'Ó Riada's Farewell', named after the composer's last recording, from Claddagh Records, the company which Montague had helped found with Garech Browne. That enterprise was a significant cultural nexus; so also was Ó Riada's with Gael Linn. Garech Browne's support was reminiscent of great house patronage from an earlier age, and the Montague sequence invokes images of Carolan. In the end it was Garech Browne who rushed Ó Riada to King's College Hospital in London in a vain attempt to save him. Other circumstantial context of the Ó Riada pieces is found in Montague's recent volume of memoir, *The Pear Is Ripe*.

The loss of friends — *Sgarúint na gCompánach* — is a universal marker on the human journey, and haunts all poets in time. Montague's sequence for Ó Riada is more than elegy however. It touches on terror and despair, reaching for some of its potency into the deep but broken Gaelic world. In 'Samhain' he references Aogán Ó Rathaille's great aisling *Gile na Gile* (Brightness of Brightness) but inverts it: 'Darkness of Darkness / we meet on our way / in loneliness . . .'

Yet the world turns. Montague survives to twice Ó Riada's span. Blessed with an unfailing gift and a steady compass, he's made four score sun-circuits and gathered in a plenteous harvest of the spirit and the word.

Herbert Street Revisted

for Madeleine

1

A light is burning late
in this Georgian Dublin street:
someone is leading our old lives!

And our black cat scampers again
through the wet grass of the convent garden
upon his masculine errands.

The pubs shut: a released bull,
Behan shoulders up the street,
topples into our basement, roaring 'John!'

A pony and donkey cropped flank
by flank under the trees opposite;
short neck up, long neck down,

as Nurse Mullen knelt by her bedside
to pray for her lost Mayo hills,
the bruised bodies of Easter Volunteers.

Animals, neighbours, treading the pattern
of one time and place into history,
like our early marriage, while

tall windows looked down upon us
from walls flushed light pink or salmon
watching and enduring succession.

2

As I leave, you whisper,
'Don't betray our truth,'
and like a ghost dancer,
invoking a lost tribal strength,
I halt in tree-fed darkness

to summon back our past,
and celebrate a love that eased
so kindly, the dying bone,
enabling the spirit to sing
of old happiness, when alone.

3

So put the leaves back on the tree,
put the tree back in the ground,
let Brendan trundle his corpse down
the street singing, like Molly Malone.

Let the black cat, tiny emissary
of our happiness, streak again
through the darkness, to fall soft
clawed into a landlord's dustbin.

Let Nurse Mullen take the last
train to Westport, and die upright
in her chair, facing a window
warm with the blue slopes of Nephin.

And let the pony and donkey come —
look, someone has left the gate open —

like hobbyhorses linked in
the slow motion of a dream

parading side by side, down
the length of Herbert Street,
rising and falling, lifting
their hooves through the moonlight.

The Great Cloak (1978)

Peter Sirr *Herbert Street Revisited*

Certain poems lodge themselves in the consciousness and stay put; become part of the obsessive anthology you take around everywhere with you, yardsticks by which you measure the effect of other poems and your own attempts to write. Sometimes the attraction is a music, a tune that won't let go, or something as happenstance as a location, an evocation of a familiar place. 'Herbert Street Revisited' certainly has these for me, with its memorable opening and slow, bittersweet movement, and the way it inhabits its different temporal zones — calling up a particular Dublin at a precise moment of its history but framing its attention to the particulars of the moment in a backward glance that also looks into the future.

The book it appears in, *The Great Cloak*, is one of the poet's finest, a beautifully orchestrated collection of lyrics on love and loss, and like the book as a whole the poem in its three distinct and carefully paced sections is subtly constructed and arranged. On one level it is a deeply intimate poem, a portrait of early marriage, but it also radiates outward to encompass the social world — the private sadness of Nurse Mullen, the smouldering bohemian glamour of Brendan Behan, the lives of animals and neighbours 'treading the pattern /of one time and place into history'. All offer an image of continuity, endurance, of our old lives somehow continuing on their own track. I love the spare economic way in which the poem achieves its effects, how the particular details are so evocative and true and somehow essential — the cat 'upon his masculine errands', Behan, the 'released bull' shouldering up the street, the pony and donkey who 'cropped flank / by flank under the trees opposite; / short neck up, long neck down' and Nurse Mullen kneeling 'by her bedside / to pray for her lost Mayo hills, / the bruised bodies of Easter Volunteers'. He evokes a whole world; the poem moves effortlessly from personal memory into a wide-angled shot of '50s Ireland. This is actually a difficult transition to achieve and Montague does it masterfully. Like the personal one, that social world is full of promise and loss: the gap between idealism and reality represented by Nurse Mullen and her cherished memories of volunteer sacrifice, the dangerous and destructive creative energy in the rampaging Behan.

In its intermeshing of public and private the poem is emblematic of his wider achievement, in that the poems are never either one or the other, but function instead as a series of layerings of different spheres of experience. We remember the epigraph to *The Great Cloak*

> *As my Province burns*
> *I sing of love,*
> *Hoping to give*
> *That fiery wheel a shove.*

The lines reconfigure the terms of an apology into a defence of a poetry of private experience, but Montague's deeper intention is to insist on the fusion of these domains. *The Rough Field* is a personal journey which, by that very insistence, ramifies into the political. This may be a very Northern kind of achievement — the poetry produced by a society whose divisions and conflicts are intimate and personal and neighbourly.

What makes the poem moving is also its act of summoning: the poet summons and celebrates his past, 'enabling the spirit to sing / of old happiness, when alone'. That act of summoning leads to the rhetorical flourish of the concluding section and, again, it is the poise and accuracy of the language that we register and admire: 'let Brendan trundle his corpse . . .', the cat as 'tiny emissary / of our happiness', falling 'soft / clawed into a landlord's dustbin', the companionable pony and donkey 'lifting / their hooves through the moonlight'. The poem is dense with telling detail, each one of which adds to its emotional weight and furnishes it with a kind of an airy and unforgettable materiality.

Edge

Edenlike as your name
this sea's edge garden
where we rest, beneath
the clarity of a lighthouse.

To fly into risk,
attempt the dream,
cast off, as we have done,
requires true luck

who know ourselves
blessed to have found
between this harbour's arms
a sheltering home

where the vast
tides of the Atlantic
lift to caress
rose-coloured rocks.

So fate relents.
Hushed and calm,
safe and secret,
on the edge is best.

The Great Cloak (1978)

Conor O'Callaghan *Edge*

There was a party in Dillon Johnston's place on Shady Boulevard in Winston-Salem, NC, the spring of 2000. There had been a book launch that night in Reynolda House. The party was a post-reading bash of faculty and significant others and pale ale. The poet Ralph Black was leaning against Dillon's carbuncle of a refrigerator in the kitchen, telling me about the expiration of his three-year contract as resident poet at Wake Forest. Instead of going back in the job market, Ralph was taking Susan and the girls the following academic year to a friend's holiday bungalow in Brittas Bay. He asked me how well I knew John Montague's poem 'Edge'. 'Not well,' I said, meaning not at all. He said the poem had become their poem, a little prayer to warm them to the thought of a winter overlooking the scrappy Irish Sea out of season. And there and then Ralph said 'Edge' from memory.

It is essentially a romantic gesture, a miniature creation myth. Its moment is the aftermath of a Tristan and Isolde elopement. The lovers have fashioned themselves a still centre surrounded by the elements' turbulence. There is an island of three stanzas run into one another and a string of internal rhymes (rest, -selves, blessed, caress, relents, best) that are struck off the poem's title. It happens like a watched wave: the swell of one sentence broken over twelve lines, the one-line sentence at the top of the last stanza that acts as a breaker, and the ensuring calm of the final three lines. The more you know it, the more impossible it feels not to read 'Edge' as a covert *ars poetica*. At the core of its great tenderness there is suffering and a note of real defiance. Its is a battle-scarred aesthetic borne of marginality, prizing out of necessity the periphery above the centre, praising placelessness over place, espousing the virtues of relative neglect as opposed to those of being famous.

Ralph and Susan are in Aix-en-Provence this winter. I can say 'Edge' from memory too. Michael Hofmann once argued that the hardest thing about being a poet is continuing to be one. When you have turned forty and have contrived to squander pretty much everything, you start to glimpse how true that might be. You know that a poet exactly twice your age — still with us, still doing it — deserves all the tributes he gets.

At Last

A small sad man with a hat
he came through the Customs at Cobh
carrying a roped suitcase and
something in me began to contract

but also to expand. We stood,
his grown sons, seeking for words
which under the clouding mist
turn to clumsy, laughing gestures.

At the mouth of the harbour lay
the squat shape of the liner
hooting farewell, with the waves
striking against Spike Island's grey.

We drove across Ireland that day,
lush river valleys of Cork, russet
of the Central Plain, landscapes
exotic to us Northerners, halting

only in a snug beyond Athlone
to hear a broadcast I had done.
How strange in that cramped room
my disembodied voice, the silence

after, as we looked at each other!
Slowly our eyes managed recognition.
'Not bad,' he said, and raised his glass:
Father and son at ease, at last.

The Dead Kingdom (1984)

Sara Berkeley *At Last*

John Montague, oft-hailed for his hauntingly simple renditions of old stories, nevertheless digs deep into human emotions with his plain style. In 'At Last' he mines the seam of father/son relations. The poem is an anecdote of meeting his father off the boat at Cobh and moving painfully through the clumsy initial greetings that speak volumes of past hurts or misunderstandings or just plain distance.

The lines 'something in me began to contract // but also to expand' describe so lucidly the conflicting and contradictory emotions that parent/child relationships so often entail. The vision of his father, 'a small sad man with a hat', coming through Customs 'carrying a roped suitcase' strikes a wistful, even pathetic note. Here is a man returning to Ireland perhaps after a long absence and he has clearly not struck gold on his travels. Montague knows he doesn't need to explain the cause of his father's sadness. We may know, but we do not need to know, that James Montague was formerly an Irish volunteer who fled to Brooklyn after involvement in ambushes and house-burnings; that he failed in business and became a subway ticket collector; that he turned to alcohol. In Montague's lexicon, the two simple adjectives and the roped suitcase say all this, and much more.

With the simultaneous contraction and expansion inside him at the sight of James, we are taken through a door from the room of the older man's disappointments to the room of the son's responses to this man: the father he barely knew from the age of four, when he (John) was sent to live with his aunts in Garvaghey, County Tyrone. The conflict of emotions is obvious, and the 'clumsy, laughing gestures' that he and his brother resort to to cover over their awkwardness seem unsurprising. But what follows is an example of Montague's deft artistry, his ability to go deeper, use the facts of scenery and surrounding to fill out and deepen the prevailing mood:

At the mouth of the harbour lay
the squat shape of the liner
hooting farewell, with the waves
striking against Spike Island's grey.

The poem turns abruptly for the drive across Ireland, where the mood seems to lighten at the 'lush river valleys' and landscapes 'exotic' to those raised in the bleaker Northern countryside. You get a sense that the drive provides both father and sons with the opportunity to relax a little after the initial tension of meeting.

And then they stop for a drink in Athlone to listen to a radio broadcast by the poet. I can only imagine the mix of feelings that led to him ensuring his father would hear this broadcast, not to mention the trepidation he must surely have felt, wondering what the response would be. The strange experience of the 'disembodied voice' is followed by a predictably pregnant silence; then, the moment of resolution, not just to the poem, but to the long years of estrangement and loneliness and wondering:

'Not bad', he said, raising his glass:
Father and son at ease, at last.

So Irish in their understatement, these are nevertheless two very healing and long overdue words. The balm at the close of this poem seems to radiate out, to try and touch every son who has ever felt betrayed or ignored or let down by his father. They are universal, they speak to the timeless human need for parental approval, and they seem in two brief syllables to wash away all the sadness, the strangeness, and the uncertainty of Montague's past with his father. Forgiveness, acceptance, even approval, at last.

Moving In

The world we see only shadows
what was there. So a dead man
fables in your chair, or stands
in the space your table now holds.
Over your hearth the sea hisses
and a storm wind harshly blows.
Before your eyes the red sandstone
of the wall crumbles, weed run wild
where three generations ago
a meadow climbed, above a city
which now slowly multiplies,
its gaunt silos, fuming mills,
strange to the first inhabitants
as Atlantis to a fish's eyes.

(*Grattan Hill*, 1974)

Mount Eagle (1988)

Bernard O'Donoghue *Moving In*

As with all major writers, on examination it emerges that Montague's thematic consistency is founded on — or reflected by — a consistency of technique and language. Even in a poem like 'Moving In', which does not look at first glance like a classic instance of this poet's subjects, the themes and their linguistic treatment echo throughout the poetic corpus. The consistency is particularly striking in this poem, I think, because it has three temporal vantage points: written in Grattan Hill in 1974; collected in *Mount Eagle* in 1988; and fitting squarely into place in the *Collected Poems* in 1995.

At first glance, on a line-count, the poem is a sonnet. But it is a short-lined sonnet, suggesting at once a further tightening of an already constricting form. Not a syllable is wasted here. The first line looks free-standing and verbless, until the turn into the second line establishes 'shadows' as the verb. Montague — again like many of the most formally gifted poets: Milton is the textbook example — is a master of enjambement; the action happens, as Donald Davie says in *Articulate Energy*, at the end of the line. But there are several other formalities collaborating in this intricate weave. There is the Irish slant-rhyme in 'there' and 'chair'; the converted verb 'shadows' is echoed by a similar syntactic usage in 'fables'. In addition the second syllable of 'shadows' echoes assonantally as a wind that blows through the poem in a semi-rhyming system: 'holds', 'Over', 'blows', 'sandstone', 'ago', 'slowly', 'silos'. In balance with this sound which blows desolately through the poem, there is the wash of the sea which 'hisses' over your hearth and reappears in the undersea city of Atlantis in the closing line. And the 'eyes' at the end are the final strand in this beautifully constructed tone-poem, sealing the vowel-music of 'wild', 'climbed', 'multiplies' and 'silos'. It is the work of a poet with a perfect ear.

Through all this there runs the familiar theme of the passage of time and the world's transience, on sea or land. But this is not a negative elegy, as is clear from the beautiful closing image. It is not an easy, Blakean fulmination against dark Satanic mills. The industrial world is 'strange' to its first inhabitants, as Atlantis was: not dismissed for its gauntness or fumes, but offering the excitement of the unfamiliar. And we see all over again the vitality of Montague's vision of the world. From the ghosts of the poem's opening, the newcomer — the 'you' addressed in the poem — takes over this world as part of 'moving in'. But each world displaces its predecessor, and the newcomer already sees the start of the process of dissolution in this world: a process which is tragic, perhaps, but which also offers an endlessly absorbing series of strangenesses. This is the poem of a supreme verbal artist who is also always alert to the tangible reality of the world and its fragility. It is another way of being grounded.

Hearth Song

for Seamus Heaney

1

The Nialls' cottage had one:
it lived under a large flagstone,
loving the warmth of the kitchen.

Chill or silent, for whole days,
it would, all of a sudden, start
its constant, compelling praise.

And all of us, dreaming or chatting
over the fire, would go quiet,
harkening to that insistent creak,

Accustoming ourselves all over again
to that old, but always strange, sound,
coming at us from under the ground,

Rising from beneath our feet,
welling up out of the earth,
a solitary, compulsive song

Composed for no one, a tune
dreamt up under a flat stone,
earth's fragile, atonal rhythm.

2

And did I once glimpse one?
I call up that empty farmhouse,
its blind, ghostly audience

And a boy's bare legs dangling
down from a stool, as he peers
through a crack in the flagstones

And here it strikes up again,
that minute, manic cellist,
scraping the shape of itself,

Its shining, blue-black back
and pulsing, tendril limbs
throbbing and trembling in darkness

a hearth song of happiness.

Mount Eagle (1988)

Rosita Boland *Hearth Song*

A friend of mine, Nollaig, once lived in an old, little, storied house in Galway, in a terraced street off Eyre Square. Most of the space in the downstairs room was composed of a cavernous fireplace, original to the house: it still had its swinging iron rod on which generations of kettles had boiled. The first time I visited her there, she said, casual as anything: 'Watch out for the cat.' Nollaig did not have a cat. She was talking about the ghost black cat that sometimes pulsed out of nothing and sat by her huge fireplace when it was alive with light. I loved the way she took for granted both the occasional presence of the ethereal cat, and the expectation that I would also do so.

'Hearth Song' is such an engaging poem because, like that spirit cat, it's about both what's present and what's absent. And what you must then imagine exists in the undefined space between these two, and the catalyst they create together.

Never named as a cricket, the 'it' that lived under a large hearthstone in the kitchen of the Nialls' cottage when John Montague was a child reminds people that it is there when it sporadically breaks into 'constant, compelling praise'. Any sound that comes from underneath carries with it a subliminal suggestion of the place where people are laid when dead. Silenced voices. Absent presences. Times past. Like a ratchet of memory, the cricket's urgent song from his hidden place makes the room quiet as people harken to the 'solitary, complusive song / Composed for no one'. Composed for no one, but heard by those who listen.

Firesides, with their endlessly original shapeshifting of flames, are places where we all dream. They are portals to the imagination. To memory. Every new fireside we sit beside in our lives is a visceral recreation of something always both new and familiar. Boy and man, the poet has watched fires; many in the company of people who are now a 'blind, ghostly audience'. The fire and the hearthside anchor him to something both essentially vital and lost forever.

Like John Montague wondering if he once saw when a boy

a 'minute, manic cellist, / scraping the shape of itself' in a flagstone crack, for years I watched out for Nollaig's cat. Late at night, once, I thought I glimpsed a feline shadow on the hearth. What did I see? I'm not sure. But I know by now just because you can't see something doesn't mean it isn't there.

This is the kinetic energy of 'Hearth Song': that tantalizing sensation of knowing you have once experienced something important, without knowing why it was so. And so, you continue to search for that eponymous 'it' again. Until, unbidden, happiness comes marvellously and insistently creaking to us, 'throbbing and trembling in darkness', even when we have almost forgotten it exists.

Border Sick Call

for Seamus Montague, MD, my brother,
in memory of a journey in winter
along the Fermanagh-Donegal border.

Looks like I'm breaking the ice!
— Fats Waller

Weary, God!
of starfall and snowfall,
weary of north winter, and weary
of myself like this, so cold and thoughtful.
— Hayden Carruth

1

Hereabouts, signs are obliterated,
but habit holds.

We wave a friendly goodbye
to a Customs Post that has twice
leaped into the air
to come to earth again
as a makeshift, a battered trailer
hastily daubed green: *An Stad.*

The personnel still smile
and wave back,
their limbs still intact.

Fragments of reinforced concrete,
of zinc, timber, sag and glint in the hedge
above them, the roof and walls
of their old working place:

Long years in France,
I have seen little like this,
même dans la guerre algérienne,
the impossible as normal,
lunacy made local,
surrealism made risk.

Along the glistening main road
snow plough-scraped, salt-sprinkled,
we sail, chains clanking,
the surface bright, hard, treacherous
with only one slow, sideways skid
before we reach the side road.

Along ruts ridged with ice
the car now rocks, until we reach
a gap walled with snow where
silent folk wait and watch
for our, for your, arrival.

The high body of a tractor
rides us a few extra yards
on its caterpillar wheels
till it also slips and slopes
into a hidden ditch
to tilt helpless, one large
welted tyre spinning.

2

Shanks' mare now, it seems
for the middle-aged,
marching between hedges
burdened with snow,

low bending branches
which sigh to the ground
as we pass, to spring back.

And the figures fall back
with soft murmurs of
'on the way home, doctor?'
shades that disappear
to merge into the fields,
their separate holdings.

Only you seem to know
where you are going
as we march side by side,
following the hillslope
whose small crest shines
like a pillar of salt,
only the so solid scrunch
and creak of snow crystals
thick-packed underneath
your fur boots, my high
farmer's wellingtons.

Briefly we follow
the chuckling rush
of a well-fed stream
that swallows, and swells
with the still-melting snow
until it loses itself
in a lough, a mountain tarn
filmed with crisp ice
which now flashes sunlight,
a mirror of brightness,
reflecting, refracting
a memory, a mystery:

Misty afternoons in winter
we climb to a bog pool;
rushes fossilized in ice.
A run up, and a slide —
boots score a glittering
path, until a heel slips
and a body measures its length
slowly on ice, starred with
cracks like an old plate.

Into this wide, white world
we climb slowly higher,
no tree, or standing stone,
only cold sun and moorland,
where a stray animal,
huddled, is a dramatic event,
a gate a silvered statement,
its bars burred with frost,
tracks to a drinking trough,
rutted hard as cement:
a silent, islanded cottage,
its thatch slumped in,
windows cracked, through which,
instead of Christians, cattle
peer out, in dumb desolation.

And I remember how, in Fintona,
you devoured Dante by the fireside,
a small black World's Classic.
But no purgatorial journey
reads stranger than this,
our Ulster border pilgrimage
where demarcations disappear,
landmarks, forms, and farms vanish
into the ultimate coldness of an ice age,

as we march towards Lettercran,
in steelblue, shadowless light,
The Ridge of the Tree, the heart of whiteness.

3

We might be astronauts creaking over the cold curve
of the moon's surface, as our boots
sink, rasp over crusted snow,
sluggish, thick, dreamlike,

until, for the first time
in half-an-hour, we see
a human figure, shrunken
but agile, an old, old man
bending over something, poking
at it furiously with a stick:
carcass of fox or badger?

'Hello,' we hallo, like strangers
on an Antarctic or arctic ice floe —
Amunsen getting a penguin! —
each detail in cold relief.

Hearing us, the small figure halts,
turns an unbelieving face, then
takes off, like a rabbit or hare
with a wounded leg, the stick its pivot,
as it hirples along, vigorously
in the wrong, the opposite
direction, away from us,
the stricken gait of the aged
transformed into a hobble,
intent as a lamplighter.

We watch as our pathfinder,
our potential guide, dwindles
down the valley, steadily
diminishing until
he burrows,
bolts under,
disappears into,
a grove of trees.

'And who might that be,
would you say?' I ask my brother
as we plod after him
at half his pace. 'Surely
one of my most urgent patients,'
he says, with a wry smile,
'the sick husband gone to get
his sicker wife back to bed
before I arrive.' And he smiles
again, resignedly.

'And besides, he wants to tidy
the place up, before the Doctor
comes. Things will be grand
when we finally get there:
he just wasn't expecting anyone
to brave the storm.

'But there'll be a good welcome
when we come.'

And sure enough all is waiting,
shining, inside the small cottage.
The fire laughs on the hearth,
bellows flared, whilst the dog rises
to growl, slink, then wag its tail.

4

My brother is led into the bedroom.
Then himself, a large-eared, blue-eyed gnome,
still pert with the weight of his eighty years,
discourses with me before his hearth,
considerately, like a true host.

'Border, did you say,
how many miles to the border?
Sure we don't know where it starts
or ends up here, except we're lost
unless the doctor or postman finds us.

'But we didn't always complain.
Great hills for smuggling they were,
I made a packet in the old days,
when the big wars were rumbling on,
before this auld religious thing came in.

'You could run a whole herd through
between night and morning, and no one
the wiser, bar the B-Specials,
and we knew every mother's son
well enough to grease the palm,
quietlike, if you know what I mean.
Border be damned, it was a godsend.
Have you ever noticed, cows have no religion?'

> *Surefooted, in darkness,*
> *stick-guiding his animals,*
> *in defiance of human frontiers,*
> *the oldest of Irish traditions,*
> *the* creach *or cattle raid,*
> *as old as the* Táin.

Now, delighted with an audience,
my host rambles warmly on;
holding forth on his own hearth:

'Time was, there'd be a drop
of the good stuff in the house,'
the head cocked sideways
before he chances a smile,
'but not all is gone.
Put your hand in the thatch
there, left of the door,
and see what you find.'

Snug as an egg under a hen,
a small prescription bottle of colourless poteen.
'Take that medicine with you for the road home.
You were brave men to come.'

5

Downhill, indeed, is easier,
while there is still strong light,
an eerie late afternoon glow
boosted by the sullen weight
of snow on the hedges,
still or bowing to the ground
again, as we pass, an iceblue
whiteness beneath our steady tread;
a snow flurry, brief, diamond-hard,
under a frieze of horsetail cloud.

The same details of field, farm
unravelling once again, as the doctor
plods on, incongruous in his fur boots

(but goodness often looks out of place),
downhill, with the same persistence
in a setting as desolate as if
a glacier had just pushed off:

> *Thick and vertical*
> *the glacier slowly*
> *a green white wall*
> *grinding mountains*
> *scooping hollows*
> *a gross carapace*
> *sliding down the*
> *face of Europe*
> *to seep, to sink*
> *its melting weight*
> *into chilly seas;*
> *bequeathing us*
> *ridges of stone,*
> *rubble of gravel,*
> *eskers of hardness:*
> *always within us —*
> *a memory of coldness.*

Only one detail glints different.
On that lough, where the sun burns
above the silver ice, like a calcined stone,
a chilling fire, orange red,
a rowboat rests, chained in ice,
ice at gunwhale, prow and stern,
ice jagged on the anchor ropes;
still, frozen, 'the small bark of my wit',
la navicella del mio ingegno.
Why could I not see it on the way
up, only on the journey home,

I wonder as my brother briefly disappears
across the half-door of another house,
leaving me to wait, as glimmers gather
into the metallic blues of twilight,
and watch, as if an inward eye were opening,
details expand in stereoscopic brightness,
a buck hare, not trembling, unabashed,
before he bounds through the frozen grass,
a quick scatter of rabbits, while
a crow clatters to the lower wood,
above the incessant cries of the sheep herd.

6

When my brother returns, breath pluming,
although he risks only a swallow,
the fiery drink unleashes his tongue:
from taciturn to near-vision,

I heard you chatting to ould MacGurren,
but the real border is not between
countries, but between life and death,
that's where the doctor comes in.

'I have sat beside old and young
on their death beds, and have seen
the whole house waiting, as for birth,
everything scoured, spick-and-span,
footsteps tiptoeing around.

'But the pain is endless,
you'd think no one could endure it,
but still they resist, taste the respite,
until the rack tightens again
on the soiled, exhausted victim.'

But the poem is endless,
the poem is strong as our weakness,
strong in its weakness,
it will never cease until it has said
what cannot be said.

The sighs and crying of someone
who is leaving this world
in all its solid, homely detail
for another they have only heard tell of,
in the hearsay called religion,
or glimpsed uneasily in dream.

'People don't speak of it,
lacking a language for this terrible thing,
a forbidden subject, a daily happening,
pushed aside until it comes in.
I remember the first time I saw it
on my first post as a *locum*.'

(That smell in the sickroom —
stale urine and *faeces* —
the old man on the grey bed,
his wife crouched in darkness.

Many generations of family
lined up along the stairs
and out into the farmyard:
the youngest barely aware

of the drama happening inside
that unblinking frame of light;
but horseplaying, out loud.
Three generations, and the tree shaking.

He has lain still for months
but now his muscles tighten,
he lifts himself into a last
bout of prayers and imprecations.

The old woman also starts up
but there is no recognition,
only that ultimate effort, before
he falls back, broken,

The rosary lacing stiff fingers.
'I did not expect to witness
the process in such a rush:
it still happens in these lost places.')

7

Just as we think we are finally clear,
another shade steps out from the shadows
(out of the darkness, they gather to your goodness),
with its ritual murmured demand:
'Doctor, would you be so good to come in?
The wife is taken bad again.'

All the clichés of rural comedy
(which might be a rural tragedy),
as he leads us along a tangled path,
our clabbery *via smaritta*.

Briars tug at us, thorn and whin
jag us, we trudge along a squelching drain;
my brother and I land ankle-deep in slush,
a gap guttery as a boghole,

and he has to haul us out by hand,
abjectly, 'Sorry we've no back lane.'

In his house, where an Aladdin burns,
we step out of our boots, socks,
before the warm bulk of the Rayburn,
and my brother pads, barefooted,
into the back room, where a woman moans.

Nursing a mug of tea in the kitchen
I confer anxiously with her cowed man.
'She's never been right since the last wain,
God knows, it's hard on the women.'

Three ragged little ones in wellingtons
stare at the man from Mars,
suck their thumbs and say nothing.
There is a tinny radio but no television.
A slight steam rises where our socks hang.
At last my brother beckons him in.

When we leave, no more conversation;
the labourer stumbling before us,
his hand shielding a candle
which throws a guttering flame:
a sheltering darkness of firs, then,
spiked with icicles, a leafless thorn,
where the gate scringes on its stone.

When we stride again on the road,
there is a bright crop of stars,
the high, clear stars of winter,
the studded belt of Orion,
and a silent, frost-bright moon
upon snow crisp as linen

spread on death or bridal bed;
blue tinged as a spill of new
milk from the crock's lip.

8

Another mile, our journey is done.
The main road again. The snow-laden car
gleams strange as a space machine.

We thrust snow from the roof;
sit cocooned as the engine warms,
and the wipers work their crescents clean

With a beat steady as a metronome.
Brother, how little we know of each other!
Driving from one slaughter to another

Once, you turned on the car radio
to hear the gorgeous pounding rhythms
of your first symphony: Beethoven.

The hair on your nape crawled.
Startled by the joy, the energy,
the answering surge in your own body.

In the face of suffering, unexpected affirmation.
For hours we've been adrift from humankind,
navigating our bark in a white landlocked ocean.

Will a stubborn devotion suffice,
sustained by an ideal of service?
Will dogged goodwill solve anything?

Headlights carve a path through darkness
back through Pettigo, towards Enniskillen.
The customs officials wave us past again.

But in what country have we been?

Collected Poems (1995)

Eiléan Ní Chuilleanáin *Border Sick Call*

I remember going with Macdara to hear John Montague read in the Physics Theatre in Earlsfort Terrace on the occasion of the launching of his *Collected Poems*: the old lecture-hall wooden, darkly marked with time. The first sight of the book: handsome, austere-looking black and white photography cover, the poet on a country road though not in winter, stretching into what might be an autumnal version of the landscape of 'Border Sick Call'.

John in person looking serious, not austere, read the poem and his voice with its slight faltering tremble, as of something made up of fragments settling, led us confidently into a world collapsing. As the uncertain textures circled us like ravens — of makeshift shacks, of snow and ice as implacable barrier, of the boundaries of small farms and empires fading duskily to nothing — there was a getting to grips:

> . . . *the so solid scrunch*
> *and creak of snow crystals* . . .

It was a journey of surprises: how the place of the poet's doctor, brother, companion, is gradually revealed, the initial refusal of the Dantesque Purgatory (which will reappear later in the vision of the icebound boat, like a cameo seal, defining, telling us that we have been where we didn't mean to go):

> . . . *no purgatorial journey*
> *reads stranger than this,*
> *our Ulster border pilgrimage*
> *where demarcations disappear,*
> *landmarks, forms, and farms vanish*
> *into the ultimate coldness of an ice age,*
> *as we march towards Lettercran,*
> *in steelblue, shadowless light* . . .

The name of the townland is one sure thing, with its literal meaning that salutes the actuality of the landscape and dismisses allegory. History is happening in the literal, with its momentary explosions, and its linguistic and geological time; it is also literary history, recalling Patrick Kavanagh's affection for the border smugglers' country of Monaghan, and Montague's own 'Like dolmens round my childhood' where 'curate and doctor trudged' to attend the aged and isolated. Another surprise: in the cold of this poem there is warmth at the centre, unlike Kavanagh's lonely satire. The travellers bring help, they come as brothers. The house the travellers find is a home of marriage and hospitality, of endurance into old age, of the fire laughing, the dog mannerly suppressing its instinctive growl. The brothers get *poitín*, and stories that go back to the *Táin Bó Cuailnge*.

If at first we saw the poem as a glittering snowy presence, its light and colour John Montague's favourite monochrome, its surface reflecting scraps of the landscape of Irish poetry (and prose, and translation) of its time, we could also hear in it echoes that prompted listening for another note, the noise of geological time which speaks in the poet's ear often at the most human moments:

> *a gross carapace*
> *sliding down the*
> *face of Europe . . .*
> *bequeathing us*
> *ridges of stone,*
> *rubble of gravel,*
> *eskers of hardness:*
> *always within us —*
> *a memory of coldness.*

But more turns of narrative, as satisfactory as a romance revelation, awaited: the vision of the boat in the descent, the sudden gracious intrusion of the hare, before the doctor's grim account of rural death, his almost proverbial summation 'the real border is not between / countries, but between life and death'.

There is another border in the poem, between the known

and the mystery. Of the *navicella* the poet asks 'Why could I not see it on the way / up, only on the journey home', and leaves the word 'home' twanging like a question to match the acceptance of limit in the final section:

> How little we know of each other! . . .

> In what country have we been?

Paths

We had two gardens.

A real flower garden
overhanging the road
(our miniature Babylon).
Paths which I helped
to lay with Aunt Winifred,
riprapped with pebbles;
shards of painted delph;
an old potato boiler;
a blackened metal pot,
now bright with petals.

Hedges of laurel, palm.
A hovering scent of boxwood.
Crouched in the flowering
lilac, I could oversee
the main road, old Lynch
march to the well-spring
with his bucket, whistling,
his carroty sons herding
in and out their milch cows;
a growing whine of cars.

Then, the vegetable garden
behind, rows of broad beans
plumping their cushions,
the furled freshness of
tight little lettuce heads,
slim green pea-pods above
early flowering potatoes,
gross clumps of carrots,
parsnips, a frailty of parsley,
a cool fragrance of mint.

Sealed off by sweetpea
clambering up its wired fence,
the goats' tarred shack
which stank in summer,
in its fallow, stone-heaped corner.

With, on the grassy margin,
a well-wired chicken run,
cheeping balls of fluff
brought one by one into the sun
from their metallic mother —
the paraffin incubator —
always in danger from
the marauding cat, or
the stealthy, hungry vixen:
I, their small guardian.

Two gardens, the front
for beauty, the back
for use. Sleepless now,
I wander through both
and it is summer again,
the long summers of youth,
as I trace small paths
in a trance of growth:
flowers pluck at my coat
as I bend down to help
or speak to my aunt
whose calloused hands
caressing the plants
are tender as a girl's.

Smashing the Piano (1999)

Aidan Rooney *Paths*

Reading 'Paths' in *Poetry* some ten years ago brought on the sort of 'take me back' attack that can easily turn an ex-pat to youtubing Van Morrison or googling for a ruin in Leitrim. It is not just Montague's unfolding and unfussy prosody that makes the correspondance visceral — *sin sin* or *sin é*, as my father would have said in a gardening moment, the pea and bean rigs staked, say, the lettuce and radish beds raked — but the poem's immediate accessibility, its Whitmanesque invitation to 'trace small paths' by the poet's side and glimpse, maybe, in the mirror, a promise on which the poem delivers.

But not before the poet gets out of the poem's way of navigating us along these paths. Here, we are off-grid in Montague kingdom with a young, would-be Nebuchadnezzar who walks us through the two gardens — first the flower, then the vegetable — of his Garvaghey boyhood, 'the front / for beauty, the back / for use'. Contrastive as the enterprise is, however, beauty and bounty are hardly exclusive, and there is as much blooming going on out the back in the potager as there is utility (nay *re*-utility) out front in the potato boiler and black pot. That sweetpea conceals 'the goats' tarred shack / which stank' no more effectively than the lilac screens an outside world of comparable husbandry. It is an incredibly busy poem. No space, not even the paths with their 'shards of painted delph', seems left unfilled, the poet mapping forth in a particular, near-precious fashion, not afraid to go anthropomorphic on the vegetables, the wonderfully accurate 'broad beans / plumping their cushions' and, equally so, 'a frailty of parsley'. Later in the poem, it is no surprise that 'flowers pluck' at the narrator's coat. There's no need really, and no room anyway, for everything to get away from itself (literally if not rhetorically), for it is a highly peopled and animaled poem too: old Lynch and 'his carroty sons'; the perfectly metonymous 'cheeping balls of fluff'; the 'marauding cat', 'hungry vixen' and 'small guardian' narrator, each left bereft of trope. Much of the achievement of the poem lies in that counterbalance of figurative and literal such that, for all its high-occupancy, the poem gets a move on, listing easily, unclaustrophobically, towards its apotheosis, with ample head-room for the reader. No stanza feels too dense. The short lines and fragments help too, and only a poet of Montague's earned nerve can open a stanza with 'With, . . .' and 'Then, . . .'

The larger guardian, of course, of the gardens *and* the narrator, is Aunt Winifred, mentioned at the outset, returned to at the end. It would be easy to declare 'Paths' essential Montague, meditative, attentive, sacral, that 'growing whine of cars' whinge tricking us back to the '70s. The gardens, however — with their wires, tar and oil-fed incubator — are hardly prelapsarian. What I admire, and what will bring me back to it, now that I keep *Smashing the Piano* within bedside reach, is not the nostalgia for an untroubled past but the discovery of an untroubled present. What lament there is is muted by that something quietly transformative occurring at the end, memory muddling youth and age, sleeplessness becoming trance. There's no need to make sense; a little blur makes perfect sense, narrator and aunt by turns returned to boy- and girlhood. Just as the gardens of beauty and use are written on his aunt's hands, at once 'calloused' and 'tender', memory translates absence into presence, empty to plenty, then to now, and then the other way about, delivering experience of its weight.

Crossroads

The dead silence
of extreme heat.

The elements for tragedy:
a country crossroads
where a young man
might meet & quarrel
with a stranger, or
take a left turn, and
land in the dungeon

(or the right, and love
the lovely princess;
my own plan, later).
Rarely, straight on.

Take that crossroads,
where three townlands
meet, Altcloghfin,
Roscavy, Rarogan,
at Garvaghey churchyard.

Mid-August, mid-'30s,
the spill of the spring
dwindles to a trickle.
The wayside flowers
are furred with dust.
Thick leaves hang.

A smell of thunder.
Few people stir out,
but young MacDonald
gets his leg under
his father's Raleigh.

He wobbles through Altcloghfin
and finds there is a cooling wind
as he freewheels down
Garvaghey's long incline

to swoop out into
the middle of the crossroads
straight into the path
of a suddenly swerving
and rubber-shredding,
furiously braking big car.

(Sam Clark had an errand.
He is driving from Belfast to Derry.
Because of the swelter
all his windows are open.
Because the road is deserted
he puts the foot down.)

News of the accident
crackles like gorsefire
through the torpid countryside:
A schoolboy killed
at Garvaghey crossroads!

Voices, anxious, loud,
call me in from the fields,
call and call, until
I come racing, racing in.
Now what have I done?
I thrust a scared face
around the byre corner
to be hailed with relief:
Thank God, you're safe.

Then go back to whack
the head off the thistles,
throw stones at the magpies
(or lie in the haybarn
and dream of the princess).

While, in the dead silence
of extreme heat, a schoolmate's
mangled body is gathered
away into an ambulance,
leaving behind the taped
and chalk-measured
scene of an accident:
a problem abandoned
on a school blackboard.

Smashing the Piano (1999)

Dennis O'Driscoll *Crossroads*

John Montague is a poet of love and loss. Exploring the 'rough field' of his home ground, he uncovers 'shards of a lost tradition' everywhere: battles bring defeat and earls take flight ('Disappearance & death / of a world'); the native language comes under threat; a time-honoured way of life is 'going, going, GONE'. Arranged inventively as a 'Loss and Gain' account, the poem 'Balance Sheet' presents Montague both as subtle celebrant of nature and trenchant satirist of so-called progress. That even love is stalked by potential loss was a lesson reinforced for the young Montague when — becoming reacquainted with his mother, who had abandoned him as a child — he was admonished not to visit her: 'I start to get fond of you, John, / and then you are up and gone.'

'Crossroads', one of two Montague poems from the 1990s which share the Mahlerian title 'Kindertotenlieder', is a profound and troubled rumination on the nature of loss itself. The warning shot triggered by the opening line's 'dead silence', the ominous early glimpse of a churchyard, and the reference to 'the elements for tragedy' prepare us to expect the worst. Anecdotal its tone may be, but this poem is not simply an atmospheric evocation of a childhood incident from the 1930s. Montague has deeper ambitions; something suspenseful — even chilling — lurks in the airless, thunder-smelling heat and desiccated landscape (parched stream, dust-furred flowers, limp leaves) as they presage the lightning bolt about to strike at the heart of a rural Tyrone community.

What strikes, actually, is a speeding car and what it collides with is a schoolboy who has freewheeled 'down / Garvaghey's long incline // to swoop out into / the middle of the crossroads'. Montague does not linger ghoulishly over the carnage, as the 'mangled body' of his schoolmate is 'gathered / away into an ambulance'. Nor is any attempt made to describe the victim, identified only as 'young MacDonald'. The bare facts deliver their own raw truths concerning the tragedy, news of which 'crackles like gorsefire' through the torpid countryside (that inspired flash of gorsefire brilliantly suggests not only the swiftness with which word spreads but also the randomness, rapidity and destructiveness of the accident itself). As relief settles over the poet's family ('*Thank God, you're safe*'), disbelief and devastation will be visited on the family whose son has been so abruptly and needlessly snatched away.

In 'Crossroads', as in Robert Frost's 'Out, Out—', a lucid, unsensational diction conveys, with buzz saw sharpness, the enormity of the tragedy and heightens the reader's awareness of the baffling arbitrariness of fate; the fragility with which the boundary line between life and death is drawn. The crossroads, where paths diverge and choices are made, presents its own balance sheet of loss and gain: 'take a left turn, and / land in the dungeon // (or the right, and love / the lovely princess . . .)'. Although Montague is far from reconciled to the dark knowledge he gleaned as a schoolboy (the memory of the wrong turn taken by 'young MacDonald' seems to have haunted the poet for sixty years), the poem is something of a reconciliation account. Impossible though it is to fully comprehend any tragedy, enigma is resolved into image, as 'the taped / and chalk-measured / scene of an accident' becomes — aptly, heartbreakingly and unforgettably — 'a problem abandoned / on a school blackboard'.

Guardians

In my sick daughter's room
the household animals gather.
Our black Tom poses lordly on
the sun-warmed windowsill.
A spaniel sleeps by her slippers,
keeping one weather eye open.
For once, they agree to differ:
nary a sound, or spit of bother.
Aloof and hieratic as guardians,
they seem wiser than this poor animal,
her father, tiptoeing in and out,
ferrying water-bottle, elixirs, fruit,
his unaccustomed stockinged stealth
tuned anxiously to a child's breath.

Smashing the Piano (1999)

Tom French *Guardians*

Up to last Christmas, under our roof, you needed something wrong with you to be reading *The New Yorker*. What changed last year was that my family gave me the gift that keeps on giving — an annual subscription. Previously, I depended on coming across it in my GP's surgery — out-of-date copies usually, read once at home by one of the midwives or interns and brought in for the waiting-room magazine rack to edify the ailing.

Reading while waiting to be called made time precious, and there was always a tricolour run up the pole and saluted — mentally, at least — when the name of one of our own appeared towards the end of the list of contributors. The poem I read that day is there, written out in my own handwriting to feel what it felt like, in the commonplace book I was keeping irregularly then, between the French navigator Cassini's 'It is better to have absolutely no idea where you are, and to know it, than to believe confidently that you are where you are not', and Paul Durcan's 'The Difficulty That Is Marriage'.

And it's only now that it occurs to me as more than coincidence, not only that John Montague's 'Guardians' should precede an eighteenth-century French navigator's paraphrase of negative capability, but that the two poems, one preoccupied with disagreeing to disagree and the other touching on agreeing to differ, should appear on facing pages.

What I loved it for the first time I read it is what I love it for, reading it again — the stealthy progress through its five sentences and fourteen lines, the combination of ordinary idiom and Northern vernacular that lives comfortably beside the bigger, more literary 'aloof' and 'hieratic', the lightness of touch, the unshowy placement of 'elixirs' between 'water-bottle' and 'fruit', the timing — how the animals are in attendance within the first couple of lines while the father's arrival is delayed until line nine, the way his arrival in the actual poem is as unobtrusive as his arrival into the imagined room, how no more is hinted at than is in the words themselves, the aptness of 'ferrying', how gradually the truth embedded in the lines yields itself up, the way — as it is with poems that hit the spot — it leaves you both surprised and delighted that such things constructed of words are possible.

Here was a writer who could do — and had done — anything, unafraid of doing the apparently simple thing that spoke directly and let you in. And now that I read it again it is 'elixirs' I am hung up on, not for the first time and not so much for the alchemical connotations but for how the word leads on to myrrh, and so transforms the cat and spaniel into scaled-down stable creatures, and the whole scene into a secular nativity.

In my commonplace book it is signed in my hand '*John Montague (The New Yorker, October '95)*'. And what I can't figure out now is how — failing total recall — I got it home and written out for rereading afterwards? In the absence of anything conclusive, the evidence points to my having left the physician's premises for the chemist's that day with more than a prescription for whatever it was that had been ailing me.

White Water

for Line McKie

The light, tarred skin
of the currach rides
and receives the current,
rolls and responds to
the harsh sea swell.

Inside the wooden ribs
a slithering frenzy; a sheen
of black-barred silver-
green and flailing mackerel:
the iridescent hoop
of a gasping sea trout.

As a fish gleams most
fiercely before it dies,
so the scales of the sea-hag
shine with a hectic
putrescent glitter:

luminous, bleached —
white water —
that light in the narrows
before a storm breaks.

Drunken Sailor (2004)

Eamon Grennan *White Water*

Something I've always admired in Montague's work is the way he insists on a slow, close, patient *looking* at things most of us might flinch from. He looks, and keeps looking, until he finds an adequately specific language for the object under his attention. 'Peer closely,' he instructs himself (and us) in one poem, 'All those small / scarlet petals are shivering.' He will not turn away from hard matters, but insists — with a mixture of fascination, sympathy, and what might be called rapt detachment — on seeing exactly what's there and then saying it in a manner that's both plain and at the same time ritualistic — formalized by line and stanza into a fixed ritual instant. It's heartening to note that in his latest work Montague has lost nothing of this courage and capacity, this willingness to *look at* and *look into* things, and to speak a materially exact and emotionally exacting truth about them, about their nature and the nature of the world as he finds it. For me the most lyrically satisfying version of this in *Drunken Sailor* occurs in the opening poem of the collection, 'White Water'.

In the first stanza of this poem it's the word 'skin' that holds my attention, bringing both factual and metaphorical levels into alignment. What the speaker sees is a feeling body. Then the difficult circumstance of the boat's existence is acknowledged, the way it manages what both supports and opposes it — the sea swell it 'rolls and responds to'. That the swell is 'harsh' accentuates *feeling* as part of the picture.

This presence of physical feeling continues in the second stanza: 'ribs' looks back to 'skin', insists on rendering the inanimate boat animate, an animation that testifies to the poet's willingness to get very close to the fact he scrutinizes. Then this body — both actual and metaphorical — is seen as the site of a 'slithering frenzy' of fish, the poet's eye getting closer as it moves through the mass of 'flailing mackerel' to the single 'gasping sea trout'. The poem's language behaves like a camera developing a scene from panning shot to close-up — the eye in unblinking action. The language prompts us to feel what is seen.

In the third stanza, then, the visual morphs into the visionary, as the imagination leaps beyond the physical into a metaphysical observation, a consideration of how death and brilliance are inextricably linked. Unconsciously evoking a line of Wallace Stevens ('death is the mother of beauty'), Montague's speaker-seer notes the gleam of the dying fish, summarizing the paradox with an oxymoron: 'putrescent glitter'.

Finally — leaving its triggering, sharply seen, material occasion behind — the poem amplifies (like a wave reaching shore) to its largest implication, having learned from its close focus on some physically disturbing facts a larger truth. This final compelling formulation, anchored in an image, enlarges our understanding of the otherwise unspeakable fusion of approaching death with a given visionary intensity: 'that light in the narrows / before a storm breaks'.

Enough to add, by way of conclusion, that this habit of Montague's reveals the overarching aesthetic of his verse to be a mix of the visual and the metaphysical. *Video ergo sum* — I see therefore I am — whatever the cost. For this brave, self-sustaining poet, a diamond clarity of seeing is, I'd hazard, as close as he can come to faith: if all things glow when they're seen as closely as he insists on seeing them, then that is 'vision' in both senses. And I wonder if this obsessive seeing might be connected with the poet's childhood sense of being *seen* by Christ, as this appears in 'Scraping the Pot', a poem about early Confession experiences. In it, the child's experience of Christ looking at him — mediated by the country phrase for Confession as *'scraping the pot'* — evolves into a state of privileged seeing: 'I saw my neighbours' souls / hanging above the hearth, / scoured and gleaming.' Being visible and vulnerable, he pushes back by means of his own calamitous (and 'confessional') clarity of seeing. At the very centre of Montague's tirelessly vigilant imagination, then, shines this clarity of sight-becoming-insight, vision becoming visionary — a marvellous, marvel-making force that for all these years has won the admiration, affection and gratitude of so many of us.

Demolition Ireland

for Sybil

Observe the giant machines trundle over
this craggy land, crushing old contours,
trampling down the nearly naked earth.
Dragon rocks dragged into the open,
dislodged from their primaeval dream.
Riverbanks, so slowly, lushly formed,
haunt of the otter and waterhen,
bulldozed into a stern, straight line;
dark trout pools dredged clean
so that doomed cattle may drink any time.
Once mysteries coiled in the tangled clefts
of weed and whin, land left to itself . . .
But see, the rushes rise again, by stealth,
tireless warriors, on the earth's behalf.

Drunken Sailor (2004)

Derek Mahon *Demolition Ireland*

It's always interesting to read Montague's prose together with the poetry: the stories, the autobiographies, *The Figure in the Cave*, where we get the back story. 'A primal Gaeltacht', he calls it in a childhood reminiscence of that title — the original landscape of Tyrone, Garvaghey and environs. 'I was brought up,' he says, 'among the hill forts of the Clogher Valley', and he recalls 'the wet lushness which excited me' after ten years abroad. Here are the sources of his erotic archaeology, his devotion to the earth as wife and mother, his ecology and politics. He invokes varieties of the incarnate Muse as identified by Robert Graves (an acknowledged Master) in *The White Goddess*. 'Do you believe in the physical presence of the Muse?' our mutual friend Desmond O'Grady once asked. (Yes of course, I replied.)

People don't talk like that any more, but it made sense to a generation born to a deeply religious culture. More often it takes a secular form. Montague's own Sean Bhean Bhocht trope, earth as woman, recurs constantly, perhaps most obviously in 'The Wild Dog Rose' but also seriatim in 'Like Dolmens', 'The Rough Field' and incidental pieces like 'Deer Park', where Boucher's sexy portrait of Marie-Louise O'Morphi, Louis XV's Irish mistress, represents the girlish beauty of Ireland as 'royal property'. This connects a seemingly decorative and exotic exercise with more local concerns and aligns it with explicitly ecological work like 'Hymn to the New Omagh Road' and 'Mount Eagle'.

'Demolition Ireland', a more recent poem, is a further addition to this line of thought. (One of the pleasures of reading Montague is to watch how things tie up.) Everything is present, or at least implicit, here. Even the dedication to his daughter ('for Sybil') seems to imply a magical dimension to this brief meditation on industrial 'development'. Again the 'naked earth' is a woman, her 'contours' to be 'trampled', her 'lushly formed' rivers and 'dark trout pools' distorted or destroyed. The coiled 'mysteries' of her 'tangled clefts' take us right back to the beginning where natural wonder mingles with sexual awe.

The poem can be read like that or be taken, superficially, as a polemic against the 'Celtic Tiger' economy we enjoyed or endured for a few brief years. The phrase, you recall, was invented by a New York financial journalist predicting rapid 'growth' for Ireland similar to that of the 'Asian Tiger'. But the species isn't native to Ireland; it has to be imported, and exported again when its time is up and the rushes, if any are left, can 'rise again'. Some think poets should leave politics alone. It's not a position to which Yeats would have subscribed — or Kavanagh, or MacNeice. Poetry, like everything else, is political in the widest sense, and it's greatly to Montague's credit that he has kept this knowledge alive. While at the same time, of course, giving us some of the finest poems we've seen in the last half-century.

Last Court

Poetry, 'tis a court of judgement upon the soul.
— Henrik Ibsen

1
Non piangere

From your last chair,
two months before that glutton, cancer,
devoured you, lawyer brother,
you gave me a final wigging, read the riot act,
as if I were some juvenile delinquent
hauled before the magistrate.

This sun-warm conservatory,
latest addition to your ultra-modern bungalow
overlooking Brown-Lecky's estate,
(now manicured golf course) recalls the deck
of that Cunard liner, the *Cameronia*,
which, ages ago, shipped us boys to Fintona.

Home again, in mid-Tyrone,
you built your now fading life,
fathering a tribe within a tribe,
only to chide me now, for my 'great mistake,
repeated, *twice*', of choosing a wife
from the wider world outside.

'They don't understand. You need somebody
who thinks like you, shares your beliefs.'
Mildly, I place a picture of your two nieces
(my Cork, French, Jewish,
Church of Ireland children)
upon your knee, for loving avuncular scrutiny.

But you sigh it away
and, having pronounced your last verdict,
stalk off to rest, dying, but striding with dignity,
without a whimper of self-pity,
through your assembled family,
your last gift, this fragile bravery.

2

To leave me forever, with your disapproval,
yet rueful love, and a contradictory testimony,
'Strangely, I have never felt so happy, as now,
giving up, letting go, floating free.'
You look down, pensively, at your glass
of burnished Black Bush whiskey.

'And, no, I no longer pray,
although I talk to God sometimes in my head.
And our parents. Why did you hurt our mother's pride
with your mournful auld poem, *The Dead Kingdom*?
Only a child, you couldn't understand their decision:
besides, you got the details wrong!'

'So you believe we'll see them again?
Bone-light, transfigured, Molly and Jim,
angels dancing upon a pin, and then
I can take it up with them again?'
'No,' you say stubbornly, 'never again,'
shaking your once-red Ulster head.

And plucking your pallid, freckled arm,
'I don't believe,' you proclaim,
'in the body's resurrection.
See how the flesh wastes parchment-thin?'

Yet, resigned as the Dying Gaul,
stoic as an ancient Roman.

3

Un grido lacerante

Dear freckled brother, in an old photo,
you throw your arm around me
in a Brooklyn park, your impulse to hug
preserved there for posterity.
Let me reverse our roles, carefully as I can,
to encircle you, this time, with *my* arm.

In far off Florence, I learnt of your death;
Evelyn calling from a rain-swept West Cork.
'It was a merciful release,' that cliché — yet true.
'But how can I trek all that way North?
My sister's children are here, as well as our own.
It's a long hard slog up to County Tyrone.'

Phone to my ear, gazing out at the Arno,
I hear, behind her, the laughter of children,
those nieces whose picture you dismissed.
'Cherish the living, while honouring the dead,
I'll stand over that, pray they'll comprehend.
The church bells of Florence will bless him instead.'

As many mourners assemble at your funeral
in our chill and distant Northern chapel
since you loved paintings I patrol
the Pitti, the Uffizi, turning from
a foam-borne Botticelli nymph, or
grave Madonna, to weep above Dante's city:

sharp-tempered, once you smashed me to the floor
in our mother's kitchen, and standing over
me, like some American boxer, 'Rise
and fight like a man' — and I only sixteen!
Aproned Molly hovering, a hapless referee;
you stalk away, to return with a brusque apology.

Sharp-tempered but kindly, you drove
your poet brother home from Dublin,
emptying my squalid flat without reproach.
Later, wives and lives came between us,
differing codes of conduct and belief.
Yet I still glimpse your ginger hair and freckle face.

Long before the cancer struck, I saw that face
grown ashen, fissured as chalk, suddenly old
as though some secret source had parched,
and sought to tell you, *Relax again*,
as when you roamed Bundoran with the Fintona gang.
But tact forbade. Or cowardice?

Now, hear my plea. Sweet-souled Santayana
might have agreed with you, brother, about exogamy,
but against your patriarchal views,
I assert the right of love to choose,
from whatever race, or place. And of verse
to allay, to heal, our tribal curse, that narrowness.

                                        Drunken Sailor (2004)

Frank McGuinness *Last Court*

When first reading *Drunken Sailor* I was very glad to come across 'Last Court', the poem in which the wise voice of John Montague salutes the great Henrik Ibsen, citing his definition of poetry as a court of judgement upon the soul. And then Montague constructs through the three acts of 'Last Court' a drama that is as deep and defiant as any of the Norwegian's strange and haunted later plays with their implacable patriarchs — men like the thieving genius, John Gabriel Borkman, or The Master Builder himself, Solness, still constructing architectural marvels to dazzle and dwarf his younger rivals, silencing the critics of the parish, sentencing the lot of us with the verdict of guilty.

Montague imbues the poem with intimate revelations, 'glass / of burnished Black Bush whiskey', 'face . . . fissured as chalk, suddenly old'. He creates two whole competing characters sharing the landscape of life history that makes them brothers in their souls as much as they are brothers of bone and blood and flesh. Yet bone, blood and flesh make profound connections — mirror images of each other, yes, but it is the concave and convex distortions of those images that touch me most. The voices are authentic by reason of their difference — the poem has a genuine capacity to defy expectations, to upstage and unsettle. The denial of the body's resurrection coming from that stern mouth is devastating, brutal as an act of fratricide.

But then the whole of 'Last Court' is one great series of devastations. In its admirably succinct biographies of generations passing it is a record of a family that from its origins sets out to disappoint itself. That is a realism I absolutely admire. I believe completely in its crisis — the choice of tact as opposed to courage. I've lived with that. So have we all. Out of his grief Montague fashions a lament for his brother which is one of his most honest love songs. 'Last Court' is a wonderful poem.

Notes

We have presented the poems in the order of their first appearance in book form and followed the texts of *Collected Poems* (1995) and more recent Gallery collections.

New Collected Poems appeared in 2012.

Thanks are due to Seamus Heaney for his special support from the beginning of this project.

For further information about the authors in this book and their Gallery publications, please visit www.gallerypress.com or contact gallery@indigo.ie